HOW TO
MOW THE LAWN

THE LOST ART OF BEING A MAN

HOW TO
MOW THE LAWN

SAM MARTIN

BLOOMSBURY
www.bloomsburymagazine.com

First published in Great Britain 2003
Bloomsbury Publishing, Plc, 38 Soho Square, London W1D 3HB

Copyright © Elwin Street Limited, 2003

Produced by Elwin Street Limited
330 / 30 Great Guildford Street
London SE1 0HS

Designed by Headcase Design
Illustrations: Paul Blow

First printing, March 2003
10 9 8 7 6 5 4 3 2 1

A CIP catalogue record for this book is available from the British Library

ISBN 0-7475-6262-8

Printed in Singapore

Disclaimer: The publisher, author and copyright holder disclaim any liability from any injury that may result from the use, proper or improper, of the information contained in this book. Please always consult an expert where necessary as we do not guarantee that the information contained herein is complete, safe, or accurate.

CONTENTS

INTRODUCTION

At about the time men started to get in touch with their feminine sides, hammer sales around the world began to drop off. At first, hardware-store owners didn't think much of it. They chalked up the downturn to the cyclic economic trends that always affect retail sales and waited for things to get better. Unfortunately, things didn't get better – they got significantly worse. Two years turned into four and four into eight. Now, some thirty years later, hammer warehouses from Bombay to Boston hold nothing but dust and broken dreams. Men, it seems, have lost the art of swinging a hammer.

On further examination, this troubling phenomenon highlights the fact that men are far worse off than simply being hammerless. Fixing a dripping tap, these days, means calling a plumber. Knowing how to make a balsamic vinaigrette has become more impressive than any knowledge of basic car maintenance. Taking a date out for a romantic dinner often stretches to little more than buying popcorn and a box of Maltesers at the cinema. Of course these activities are still resourceful – men have always been that. The problem is that they just aren't very manly.

At least, not in the same way Sir Richard Burton, the 19th-century British explorer, was manly. He was so tough he managed to sleep in a tent literally for years. During this time he suffered a spear in the face, he sweated out a case of life-threatening malaria and almost reached the source of the river Nile. And then, after all that, he still managed to head home and write a best-selling book about it.

You don't find too many smooth operators like Bogart and Brando around these days either. Men like that were gentle enough to out-charm a cobra while being principled enough to land a hard right to the jaw of any man who would say otherwise. Nowadays, most men no longer know what it takes to be a real man.

So what does it take for a man to recover that combination of toughness and charisma? For some it takes being able to grow a beard, while others need to display a certain rapport with women. For me, who was raised by women and grew up having to rely on friends' fathers and the cinema for good male role models, it took eight long, hard months camping in the forests of Ontario and British Columbia, Canada, and planting trees – nearly 80,000 of them. During that time I slept in a tent, cut off all my hair, eschewed the company of women and became intimately acquainted with hard work and dirt – the two things, I have learned, that real men aren't afraid of.

So whatever it takes for a man to recoup his manhood, it is a certainty that work and dirt will play a role along the way. After all, a man who comes home dirty (whether with motor oil on his hands or coffee stains on his shirt) is a man who's been out in the world. But being a man also takes a certain amount of fearlessness. No one ever got to the top of Mount Everest by staying at home, and reaching the summit didn't happen on anyone's first attempt. A real man knows that there's a great deal to learn from failing completely.

Inside these pages you'll find an indispensable guide to all things manly, whether it involves fixing the car or the perfect cocktail, climbing a mountain or removing a splinter. There are instructions for do-it-yourself projects that will get you dirty, tips on how to shave (or not) and advice on how to get on or off your feet with a date. A section on the great outdoors will teach you to embrace the natural world, whether you have to mow it or survive in it until the search party arrives. You'll even come away knowing a few things about how to be a hero, the dream of any real man worth his salt.

So, although they don't make men like they used to, they shouldn't really have to anymore. There are plenty of us here already. All we need is a little guidance – and a good hammer.

THE
GREAT
OUTDOORS

Ah, the great outdoors. This is one of the few places that can make a tough guy even tougher. All you have to do is mow an acre of saint augustine grass in August, grill steaks for twenty hungry guests, and get lost in the woods for five days—and come out in one piece. That way you'll roughen up your hands. Men are proud of their rough hands. Women like them too: they're a sign that you're not a stranger to fresh air and a little dirt.

HOW TO MOW THE LAWN

When the time comes to buy yourself a lawn mower, get on a serious pair of work boots and head on down to the showroom to kick the tyres on a few of these beauties.

ROTARY MOWER: Push-and-walk-behind rotary mowers are the most popular choice for lawns of around $1,000yd^2/800m^2$, and may come with a power-drive mechanism that propels the machine for you.

REEL MOWER: These cut the grass using a cylindrical north–south-spinning set of blades. Although they can be run on petrol, a real man would opt for the man-powered model.

ELECTRIC MOWER: An electric mower uses a standard engine with an extension cord. The problem is that, in hauling the power cord all over the lawn, you have to be careful not to hack it to bits or lose composure.

MEGA MOWER: Nothing beats a mower you can ride. Plus, if your car breaks down on Saturday night, you can practically pick up your date in one of these babies. However, you'll look decidedly unmanly rumbling around the garden unless you have at least half-an-acre's worth of grass.

DO'S AND DON'TS

☒ Don't mow wet grass. The lawn will not be cut evenly.

☑ Do sharpen the mower blade before each mowing season. Dull blades shred the top of the grass, leaving frayed ends that will dry out and turn brown.

☑ Do change the pattern each time to avoid wearing wheel marks into the lawn.

MOWING TECHNIQUES

Mowing with your shirt off can be a catch-22. On the one hand, grass clippings are going to leave you itchy. On the other, you will always impress the girl next door with a one-two punch of hard work (the actual mowing) and bare chest (va va voom!).

You will need	**H O W T O**
lawn mower	1. Mow around the perimeter of the lawn.
roller	2. Work back and forth across the lawn in strips You can work parallel to the house or at a 90- or 45-degree angle. Overlap the strips slightly.
time	
energy	3. Go over the mown strips with a roller. Rolling bends the grass, creating light and dark stripes as you roll in one direction and then the other.

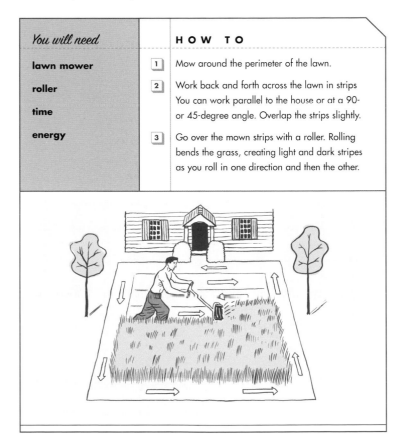

GARDEN BASICS

Which plants will grow in your area (technically, what hardiness zone are you in)? Where in the garden should the plants go? How much water do they need? Most of this information can be obtained from your local garden nursery. Generally, however, the best time to plant is in spring, once the last freeze has come and gone. Plants need a lot of water when they first go in and daily watering through the hot summer months. Usually, it is best to water in the early morning rather than at night.

LAYOUT

It makes sense to plan what goes where in the garden before getting started. This will guarantee results that make everything look sharp and inviting – you included. Shrubs or flowerbeds can be used to frame the front of the house, while a row of trees acts as a screen against busy streets or peeping neighbours – essential for maintaining that all-over tan in privacy.

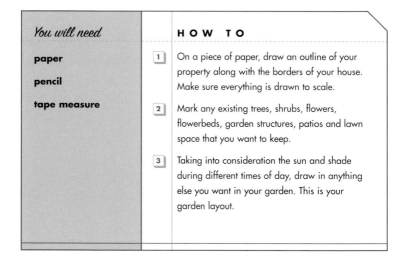

You will need	HOW TO
paper	**1** On a piece of paper, draw an outline of your property along with the borders of your house. Make sure everything is drawn to scale.
pencil	
tape measure	**2** Mark any existing trees, shrubs, flowers, flowerbeds, garden structures, patios and lawn space that you want to keep.
	3 Taking into consideration the sun and shade during different times of day, draw in anything else you want in your garden. This is your garden layout.

GROWING THINGS

Men who grow things successfully are saying two things to the women in their lives: I care, and, I can do many different things with my hands. By combining their nurturing, fatherly side with a burly, outdoorsman's know-how, men who are proficient in the garden are simply impossible to resist.

GROWING VEGETABLES

This might seem a bit domestic at first, but it is a good idea. No woman can ignore a man who slams his courgette on the kitchen table and tells her it's home-grown.

You will need		**H O W T O**
rectangular, sunny plot of land	1	Remove any grass, sod or rocks from the area with a shovel.
shovel	2	Fire up the rotary tiller (or use a pitchfork) and churn up the soil in the plot.
rotary tiller		
garden hoe	3	With a garden hoe, and following the directions on the seed packets, dig shallow rows of trenches that run east–west about 6in/15cm apart. Mound excess dirt alongside the trenches.
packets of vegetable seeds		
watering can	4	Sprinkle a row of seeds along the length of the trench, and press them lightly into the soil with your finger.
water		
	5	Fill in the trench with the dirt alongside and lightly water each row.
	6	Mark what crops you plant on a label and place it in the dirt at the end of each row.

PLANTING A TREE

Nothing says "I'm here for the long haul, honey" more explicitly than planting a tree. Then again, you might just need a good windbreak.

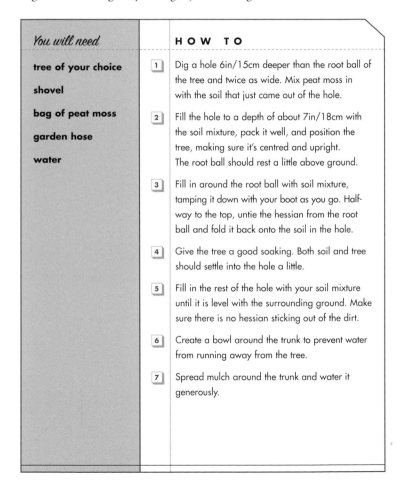

You will need

tree of your choice

shovel

bag of peat moss

garden hose

water

HOW TO

1. Dig a hole 6in/15cm deeper than the root ball of the tree and twice as wide. Mix peat moss in with the soil that just came out of the hole.

2. Fill the hole to a depth of about 7in/18cm with the soil mixture, pack it well, and position the tree, making sure it's centred and upright. The root ball should rest a little above ground.

3. Fill in around the root ball with soil mixture, tamping it down with your boot as you go. Half-way to the top, untie the hessian from the root ball and fold it back onto the soil in the hole.

4. Give the tree a good soaking. Both soil and tree should settle into the hole a little.

5. Fill in the rest of the hole with your soil mixture until it is level with the surrounding ground. Make sure there is no hessian sticking out of the dirt.

6. Create a bowl around the trunk to prevent water from running away from the tree.

7. Spread mulch around the trunk and water it generously.

DO'S AND DON'TS

X Don't grab a young tree by its trunk when you're moving it around. You might damage the roots. Grab it by its root ball instead.

✓ If you're afraid the wind might blow your tree over, drive two 6-ft/1.8-m long, 1x2in/2.5x5cm stakes into the ground on either side of it and tie them loosely to the tree trunk with thick-gauge wire. To prevent the wire from cutting into the young tree thread it through pieces of old garden hose.

LAYING A CONCRETE PATIO

Laying your own patio is a simple job that will keep your guests comfortable (and off the lawn you spent all summer mowing). It will also do much to bolster your DIY initiative and prowess. Better still, it allows you the perfect opportunity to show off at the time-honoured male ego-fest that is the barbecue!

You will need		**H O W T O**
concrete paving slabs	1	Stake out the patio area and use a shovel to dig out the soil to a depth of about 6in/15cm. Tamp it down firmly with a hand or power tamper.
shovel		
hand or power tamper	2	Fill in 3in/7.5cm worth of crushed granite. (To prevent spilled beer from pooling on or under the finished patio, gently slope it by $1/8$in per foot/$1/2$cm per 30cm. Tamp it down as you go.)
crushed granite		
sand	3	Fill in 2in/5cm of sand on top of the granite, and screed the sand into a smooth base.
4-ft/1.2-m level	4	Lay the concrete slabs, leaving $3/4$in/2cm between each one. Use a hammer and chisel to cut any slabs to fit once all of the whole ones have been laid.
hammer and chisel		
broom		
	5	Pour more sand on top of the slabs and sweep it into the gaps with a broom.

BARBECUING

Holding a bloody hunk of meat over an open fire has been a man's job since it was first decided to hunt for dinner rather than pick it off a bush. And while most men no longer butcher their own supply, barbecuing meat is still at the top of your job description.

WHAT KIND OF BARBECUE?

If you don't have the time or space to stack a bunch of bricks together for your own back-garden barbecue pit, head down to your local outdoor store and find a model to take home and fire up.

PROPANE BARBECUE: All you have to do here is turn a knob to get the gas flowing, press a button to spark the fire and toss the steak on the grill – no coal, no newspaper, no lighter fluid.

CHARCOAL BARBECUE: This is more messy and comes with the sense of having built a fire in the wild to cook the game you just hunted down.

SMOKER: Smoking meat is impressive stuff. You have to keep the fire going for up to 12 hours while a joint cooks slowly and surely.

H I N T

✓ While you're at it, don't miss the opportunity to buy a few extras. You'll need a wire brush to clean the metal grate, and tongs and spatulas for turning the meat. A charcoal chimney starter is a good way to light a barbecue without using lighter fluid, although a real man would consider this cheating.

BUILDING A BARBECUE PIT

Building something with bricks is a job that will put hairs on your chest. And what better way to start than to build your own barbecue pit?

You will need		**HOW TO**
two metal barbecue grills	1	First, go and buy your barbecue grills and coal tray. Whatever size you choose will determine the size of the pit. Then calculate the number of bricks you'll need. My pit is 13 courses high at the sides with three more courses at the back for a wind block. One side and the back are both three courses deep. The other side is nine.
iron tray to hold the coals and ashes		
chalk line	2	If you already have a patio, find an area where a barbecue pit will not burn down the house (see Fig. A). If you don't have a patio, you'll have to build one. (A flat spot on your lawn is not level or sturdy enough to support the weight of barbecue pit, even if it is immaculately mowed.)
standard masonry bricks		
pointed trowel		
mortar	3	Measure out the perimeter of the pit and snap chalk lines to use as guides. Do a test run with the first course of bricks by laying them down on the slab, leaving 1/2in/1cm between each brick to compensate for the mortar.
hand level		
reinforcing bar		
	4	Remove the bricks and, with your trowel, put down a layer of mortar. Set the first bricks inside the chalk lines, remembering to add mortar to their sides as you go.

continued on next page

continued

5 Stack each course of bricks on top of the one before it, mortaring and cleaning the brick faces as you go (see Fig. B). Use a hand level to check for level and plumb as you build.

6 When you get to the eighth course, embed lengths of reinforcing bar in the mortar so that about 4in/10cm of it sticks out into the centre of the pit. Do the same for the ninth and 12th courses (see Fig. C). These will be the supports for your two grills and the coal tray (see Fig. D).

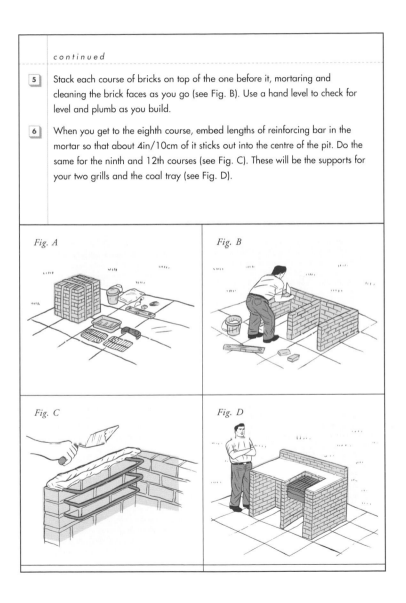

Fig. A

Fig. B

Fig. C

Fig. D

WHAT TO BARBECUE

When men think of cooking outdoors, they think meat, and that's because meat tastes good. The best cuts of meat to barbecue are the thinner, smaller ones like pork chops, chicken legs, ribs, flank or sirloin steaks, rib-eyes or T-bones. Before flopping any meat on the grill, though, think about rubbing it down with some spices or marinating it for a few hours. Garlic, shallots and fresh herbs combine with red wine to make a good beef soaker, for example. At the very least, don't forget those old, no-flair standbys, salt and pepper. A little dash here and there really does make a difference.

BUCK'S TEXAS STEAK RUB

Like all good Texas men, my grandfather Buck had a wardrobe full of cowboy boots, a hat for every occasion and a taste for good-quality beef. He was also King of the Grill, and, before any meat touched the metal grill, he'd always rub it down with a secret concoction of spices and oils.

You will need		HOW TO
two teaspoons garlic salt	1	Mix all the ingredients in a bowl to form an oily rub.
one teaspoon black pepper	2	Press the rub into the meat and let sit for an hour.
	3	Fire up the charcoal.
two tablespoons lemon juice		
five tablespoons olive oil		

BARBECUE STANCE

Legend has it that John Wayne grilled up 60 pounds of rib-eyes for the entire cast and crew of *True Grit* without putting down his tongs or leaving the barbecue unattended once.

Take a page from The Duke's book of barbecuing protocol and learn how to be smooth but stern while manning the pit. Make no mistake – the physical act of cooking outdoors is as important to your stature as a man (and by extension as a hunter/provider) as mowing the lawn.

First, decide on an imaginary perimeter around the barbecue pit and call it yours, even if you're away from home (men adapt). Let no one enter. Then, before you fire up the charcoal, get all the tools you need within arm's reach and make sure there's someone near to bring you more beer. Leaving your station at any time is out of the question. Once the cooking is well under way, adopt the classic barbecue stance. Stand with your legs apart, knees slightly bent, beer in one hand and tongs, slightly raised and at the ready, in the other. Don't let go of the tongs until the last burger has been served.

OUTDOOR SURVIVAL

If you're planning on spending time outdoors – like in a tent, where you're far enough away from most things that resemble civilization – it's good to be prepared for the worst. After all, there's always the chance you'll get lost on a hike or stuck on the side of that mountain you happen to be climbing.

Even if you're not planning on spending some time outdoors, but you find yourself doing just that anyway (hurricane trashes the house, girl-friend locks you out…), there are a few things you'll want to know in order to, say, survive. Building a fire is one, fending off animals is another.

ESSENTIAL EQUIPMENT

As with many things manly, preparation starts with gear. The following is a list of equipment that should be taken with you when you go camping.

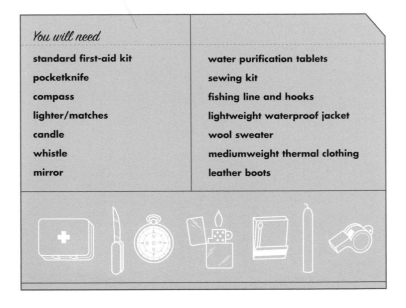

You will need

standard first-aid kit

pocketknife

compass

lighter/matches

candle

whistle

mirror

water purification tablets

sewing kit

fishing line and hooks

lightweight waterproof jacket

wool sweater

mediumweight thermal clothing

leather boots

FINDING WATER

While you may be hungry enough to eat a horse, it's always best to find water first. A man can last up to 10 days without food, but a day or two without water is bad news. Finding water is mostly about looking in the right places.

You will need	**WHAT TO DO**
rubber hose	**1** Fresh water collects in rock crevices and tree hollows. If you have a rubber hose, siphon the water out or use some kind of dipper to scoop it out. If the water is difficult to retrieve without spilling, dip a cloth into the water until it is saturated and then wring it out over a container.
cloth	
container	
water purification tablets	**2** Purify any water you collect with purification tablets or boil it over a fire for three to five minutes.
knife or machete	**3** Ice and snow are good, but eating either without melting it first can lower valuable body temperatures and cause diarrhoea.
	4 Cacti are a good source of water. Just cut off the top to access the pulp and squeeze the water out into a container.
	5 Bamboo collects water. If you find some, bend the top of one stalk over a container for water to drain out.
	6 Banana trees are also a good source of water. Cut the tree off about 6in/15cm above the ground and dig out a bowl in the stump, where water will collect from the tree's roots.

FORAGING FOR FOOD

When you're in a forest or jungle, it may seem like there's plenty to eat, and there is. You just have to know what you're looking for so you don't poison yourself.

WHAT'S GOOD TO EAT

- ✓ Algae, moss and lichens are good to eat but supposedly don't taste very nice. If you find some algae, wash it in fresh water and boil it to form a protein-rich jelly.

- ✓ Nuts are great to eat if you can find them.

- ✓ Berries are good. Just make sure they are blue or black. Red ones are strictly off-limits.

- ✓ Grasshoppers, crickets, termites, fly larvae, grubs, slugs, maggots and worms are unfortunately good to eat. Just cook them first, perhaps as a stew. They can be found under logs, on dead animals and in swampy areas around water.

- ✓ Ants. They contain a lot of sugar and should be eaten alive.

- ✓ Moths, caterpillars and scorpions. (Don't eat the stinger.)

- ✓ Dandelions, including the root and flower.

- ✓ The inner bark of pine and birch trees, which are soft and chewy.

- ✓ Pine needles make good tea.

- ✓ Seaweed is high in vitamin C and other minerals that are good for you. Find fresh seaweed rather than any that has been washed up on the beach.

WHAT'S BAD TO EAT

- ❌ Anything red.

- ❌ Dead insects.

- ❌ Mushrooms. Not only are they lacking in nutrition, but many types are poisonous.

- ❌ Brightly coloured caterpillars are also poisonous.

- ❌ Anything that smells of almonds (which means it contains cyanide).

- ❌ Anything with a sharp, bitter or burning taste.

- ❌ Anything with a milky, rubbery sap.

- ❌ Any five-segmented fruit.

- ❌ Anything that is spoiling, mildewed, old or dried out.

- ❌ Most beans or seeds inside pods.

- ❌ Plants with three leaves.

HINTS

- ✔️ Although you shouldn't eat mushrooms, you can usually find water where they grow – in crevices among rocks or in hollows of trees.

- ✔️ If you think you've eaten something poisonous, drink lots of water and make yourself vomit.

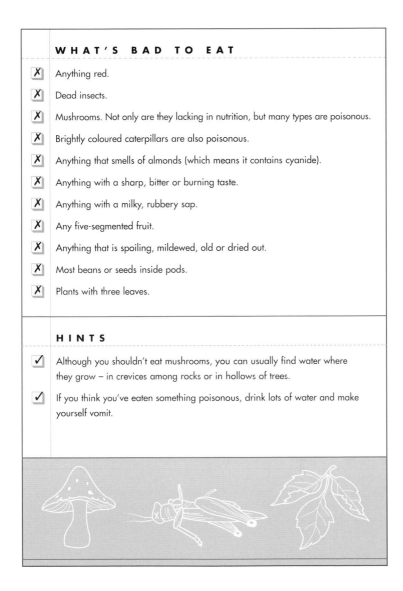

HOW TO BUILD A FIRE

For a fire to burn – and stay lit – you need plenty of fuel (wood, newspaper, an old pair of socks). Gather plenty of wood in advance to avoid tramping through the pitch black to get more. Hardwoods, like oak, burn the hottest and longest while green woods burn bright and fast.

You will need	**H O W T O**
shovel, stick or other digging device **rocks, large and small** **hard, dry wood** **matches or lighter**	**1** Choose a spot that is relatively out of the wind and where there are no overhanging branches or dry grasses. Dig a shallow, round pit roughly 6in/15cm deep and 3ft/90cm in diameter. Place large rocks around its circumference (see Fig. A). **2** In the middle of the pit make a small but tight tepee of kindling using dry grass, twigs, sticks, bark – anything that might catch fire easily. Build it up about 12in/30cm high (see Fig. B). **3** Find two bigger logs and place them parallel to each other on either side of the tepee. Stack two slightly smaller logs on top of them to create a square (see Fig. C). Repeat this process two more times until you have a square pyramid of progressively smaller logs surrounding the kindling. **4** Using matches or a lighter, set the tepee alight. Place further sticks and branches inside the wood pyramid as the fire begins to burn hot (see Fig. D).

DO'S AND DON'TS

☑ Do make the fire pit small and compact. The rocks will serve to keep the wind off and will act like an oven, radiating the heat more effectively.

☑ Do be sure and plan thoroughly if you're stuck somewhere and you're going to use up your last matches starting the fire. You don't want this fire to go out. Get plenty of wood to burn and find a way to keep it dry.

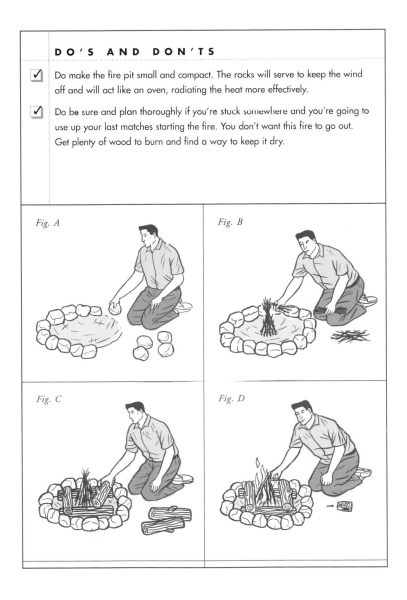

Fig. A

Fig. B

Fig. C

Fig. D

STARTING A FIRE
WITHOUT MATCHES

If you don't happen to have a lighter or some dry matches with you, then all is not lost: there are other ways to start a fire. You can try getting a spark with flint and steel, or use a magnifying glass to focus a concentrated ray of sunlight on to a dry nest of tinder. Failing that you can do it the really difficult way: by rubbing two sticks together.

You will need	HOW TO
straight stick of hardwood (the drill)	**1** Whittle one end of the drill into a point and round off the other end.
flat piece of dry, dead, softwood (the fire board)	**2** Cut a small hole halfway along the fire board and about 1in/2.5cm from its edge. The hole should be big enough to allow the rounded end of the drill to fit inside.
hand-sized piece of hardwood (the socket)	**3** Then cut a triangular notch in the fire board from the hole to the nearest edge. This will serve as a channel for ashes and embers to spill out and onto your kindling.
bootlace	
1¹/₂-ft/50-cm-long slightly bent stick (the bow)	**4** You are going to use the socket to press down firmly on the drill. To stop it from slipping, cut a small hole in the socket so that the pointed end of the drill will fit there snugly.
dried grass, pine needles and twigs for kindling	**5** Tie your bootlace loosely onto each end of the bow so that you'll be able to loop it over the drill.
	continued on next page

continued on next page

continued

6 Rest the fire board on the ground so that the notched side is in contact with a small, but tight, nest of kindling. Place the round end of the drill in the hole in the fire board and hold it in place firmly with the socket.

7 Make sawing motions with the bow to work the drill back and forth in a not-too-fast, not-too-slow, steady rhythm. Make sure the drill stays in contact with the fire board. Eventually, the friction will cause smoke to form and embers should start rolling down the notch and into the nest of kindling.

8 When this happens, add more dried grass to the pile of kindling and blow gently to ignite the ember into flames. Then work quickly and carefully to build up the fire.

HINT

✗ Don't get discouraged as this can take a long time to accomplish. The good thing is you'll get nice and toasty from all the exercise.

DO'S AND DON'TS

✗ Don't forget to collect plenty of firewood before you start trying to get an ember.

FINDING YOUR WAY IN THE WOODS

There's no shame in getting lost. Some of the most adventurous men in history have done it (think of Columbus). What will blemish your image as an outdoorsman, though, is not being able to find your way home.

HOW TO

1. Before setting out, get a simple bearing of the direction you start off on and try to keep track of the direction you're heading in. Use the sun as a guide.

2. Get a map of the terrain and note some major landmarks – bridges, cabins or streams you will be encountering along the way. Once you reach one of them, get the map out again and check your position.

3. Be alert to the sights, sounds and smells of the terrain as you walk. Look behind you to see what the terrain will look like on the return trip.

4. Stop periodically and use a compass to check your direction.

5. If you're lost, you don't have a compass and the sun is out, you can drive a straight stick into a flat area of ground and mark the end of the stick's shadow. Then wait to see which direction the stick's shadow travels in. It will always travel east to west.

HINT

☑ To use a compass, it's important that you stay away from iron and other magnetic things as they will skew the reading. Pocketknives, tools, stoves, batteries and electronic equipment should be at least 6ft/1.8m away when you take a compass reading.

FINDING YOUR WAY
IN THE SUBURBS

Getting lost in the burbs is easier than you might think, especially if all the houses look the same and the street names start to sound similar (Cedar Drive, Hazelnut Grove, Walnut Hill). You could pull over and get out your compass but you run the risk of looking like an idiot, especially if you happen to be on a date. And it is just as bad if you have to stop at a petrol station to ask where on earth you are. It's best to try and find your way home by using your expert powers of deduction.

HOW TO

1. Just as you would when heading into the wilderness, make sure you know which direction you're driving in when you set off for the suburbs. When you make turns, mentally adjust the direction.

2. In any town, there are major north–south and east–west arterial roads and most of the time you can tell which way they run by seeing where the sun is in the sky (it rises in the east, sets in the west and travels across the southern sky).

3. Also, make a note of major landmarks like fast-food restaurants or petrol stations and use them to guide yourself back home.

HINT

✓ Using the sun as a guide can be tricky in countries of the southern hemisphere. Just remember that while it still rises in the east and sets in the west, it will travel across the northern sky as it does so.

HOW TO DEFEND YOURSELF AGAINST WILD ANIMALS

There's always a chance you'll run into animals out in the wilderness. On the one hand (the one holding the shotgun) this a good thing – especially if the animal appears to have juicy flanks and you're hungry. On the other hand (the one that forgot to pack any weapons), it can be bad – especially if the animal in question has teeth or claws. The best plan is to find out about the animals you might run into and prepare yourself.

BEARS: Unless they are surprised, or protecting their bear cubs, bears aren't usually aggressive towards humans. If you run across a black bear back slowly away from it, waving your hands, yelling or blowing that whistle you packed. Usually it will wander off. Waving at, and jumping up and down in front of, a grizzly bear, however, will do the exact opposite. In this case your only hope may be to play dead.

BIG CATS: If you happen to stumble into a big cat, the worst thing you can do is turn around and run. Cats always pounce on and attack their victims from behind. It's better to turn and face the cat and start waving your hands, yelling or blowing that whistle.

SNAKES: Most snakebites occur when humans stumble on a snake and startle it. The best way to prevent this is to be cautious when walking around and sitting on logs in areas with high snake populations.

ELEPHANTS: Unless you're in Africa or India, you are unlikely to run into an elephant or two while on a casual outing in the bush. But if you do, and the beast starts charging after you, the best option is to stand absolutely still. Most elephant charges are bluffs and if they can see that you're not impressed with their size, flapping ears and loud snorts then they'll go back to pruning the surrounding trees.

HINT

☑ If you do get bitten by a snake, do not cut open the wound with a knife. Simply suck a shallow wound for about five minutes, spitting out the venom. If it appears to be a deeper bite, keep the wound below your heart, loosen any constrictive clothing, and get yourself to a hospital.

MEN
AND
MACHINES

Real men are those who are totally self-subsistent, epitomized by knowing how to fix a car—or at least parts of a car, since pride will also tell a man to avoid any undue hardship and get someone else to fix the really tricky bits. The same goes for motorcycles and bicycles. If you can fix it for yourself, you don't ever have to worry about walking to work again.

UNDER THE BONNET

Look under the bonnet of any car and you'll see the same thing: an internal combustion engine. Some may be bigger than others but they all work on the same principle. The main work of any engine takes place within the engine block inside the cylinders. There, spark plugs (Fig. A) ignite petrol and air (allowed into the cylinders by valves), causing pistons (Fig. B) to move up and down with each tiny explosion (the combustion part). The action of the pistons turns the car's crankshaft (Fig. C), which turns the wheels and makes the car go. Everything else under the hood – the tubes, fans, belts, wires and other hunks of metal – help the cylinders do their job.

HOW TO TALK TO A MECHANIC

Although there are plenty of honest, hard-working mechanics who will tell you exactly what's wrong with your car and then fix it without any tomfoolery, there are those who might want to make an extra quid here or there by telling you your car needs a new fan belt, for example, when it really only needs a tune up. To prevent such grief in your life, get to know a bit about your car. That way, when you do talk to a mechanic, you can speak a language he will understand… and respect. Above all, never tell a mechanic what you think needs to be done to the car and always get a written estimate before any work starts.

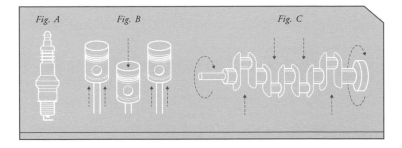

Fig. A   Fig. B   Fig. C

BASIC CAR MAINTENANCE

A good set of tools does not automatically get you a trouble-free car. You have to get under the bonnet and actually use that socket set, instead of just talking about it. But if you can manage the basic upkeep yourself, you'll save money by not having to get a mechanic to do the simple stuff.

CHECKING AND CHANGING THE OIL

Oil helps lubricate the pistons as they move up and down inside the cylinders.

You will need		HOW TO
rag	1	The car must have a cold engine. Locate the dipstick – usually on one side of the engine.
appropriate weight oil for your car	2	Pull it out and wipe it off with your rag. Put it back in as far as it will go and pull it out a second time.
funnel	3	The oil level will show on the end of the dipstick.
	4	If it appears low, unscrew the oil filler cap on top of the engine and, using a funnel, pour in 2 pints/1 litre of oil.
	5	Check the level of oil again with the dipstick.

	DO'S AND DON'TS
X	Don't overfill the oil in the engine. Your car will emit a white smoke if you do and gaskets might break, leaking oil everywhere.

CHANGING THE SPARK PLUGS

One of the most satisfying and easy ways to look as if you know what you're doing under the bonnet is to change the spark plugs. It's a job you should do every two years or 30,000 miles/50,000 kilometres, whichever comes first, and the engine will purr like a kitten when you've finished.

You will need	**H O W T O**
ratchet wrench with $3/8$-in/95-mm spark plug socket	1 Make sure the engine is "cold" before you start.
	2 Locate the spark plugs in the engine block. To avoid mixing up spark plug wires and corresponding spark plugs, do one at a time.
new set of spark plugs	3 Remove the wire from a spark plug by grabbing its boot – the angled rubber end that actually fits over the spark plug – and pulling it straight off.
rag	4 Use a rag to wipe down the exposed spark plug and the area around it.
	5 Remove the spark plug by fitting the $3/8$-in/ 95-mm socket and ratchet wrench over the spark plug and turning anticlockwise.
	6 Make sure the cylinder threads are clean and screw the new spark plug in by hand. Once you've turned it as far as it will go by hand, use the ratchet wrench and socket to tighten it firmly.
	7 Replace the spark plug wire and repeat the steps for the rest of the spark plugs.

D O ' S   A N D   D O N ' T S

☒ Don't over-tighten a new spark plug. It can break in half fairly easily.

TOUCHING UP DENTS AND SCRATCHES

Dents can be hammered out by banging gently on the underside of the dent while holding a scrap of wood or metal against the exposed side.

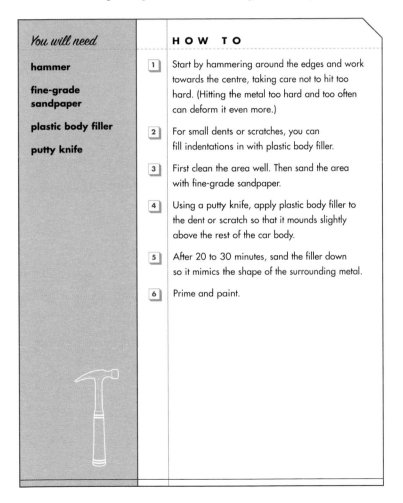

You will need

hammer

fine-grade sandpaper

plastic body filler

putty knife

HOW TO

1. Start by hammering around the edges and work towards the centre, taking care not to hit too hard. (Hitting the metal too hard and too often can deform it even more.)

2. For small dents or scratches, you can fill indentations in with plastic body filler.

3. First clean the area well. Then sand the area with fine-grade sandpaper.

4. Using a putty knife, apply plastic body filler to the dent or scratch so that it mounds slightly above the rest of the car body.

5. After 20 to 30 minutes, sand the filler down so it mimics the shape of the surrounding metal.

6. Prime and paint.

CHANGING A TYRE: CAR

Getting a flat tyre in the middle of nowhere is bad. Not knowing how to change it is worse. This is one of the basics every man should know. And remember: it is not uncommon for a grown man to stand on the wheelbrace to loosen and tighten nuts, so don't hesitate to do this if necessary.

You will need		**HOW TO**
flathead screwdriver	1	Remove spare tyre, wheelbrace, jack and screwdriver from the trunk.
wheelbrace	2	If you have a hubcap, use the screwdriver or the flat end of your wheelbrace to prise it off.
jack		
spare tyre	3	Use the nut key on the wheelbrace to loosen the wheel nuts on the flat tyre. Once you've loosened the first nut, do the nut directly opposite, and so on, but do not remove them yet.
	4	Place the jack near the tyre you're changing. (Most owner's manuals show the right placement.)
	5	Jack up the car until there's enough room to remove the flat tyre and replace the spare.
	6	Remove the wheel nuts from the flat tyre and pull the tyre off.
	7	Replace with spare. Lower the car and tighten the wheel nuts.

TIP

✓ In general, you loosen a nut by turning it anticlockwise. If the nut is to be turned clockwise there will be an R on the nut.

JUMP-STARTING

It seems like a cruel joke that, with all the complex things that can go wrong in a car, simply leaving the lights on does it every time.

You will need	**H O W T O**
jumper cables **second car**	**1** Align the second car with the dead one so that the batteries are close to each other. Turn off the second car.
	2 If both batteries are not cracked or leaking, get out your jumper cables and attach the red (positive) clips to the positive post on each battery (second car first).
	3 Next, place the black (negative) clips onto the negative posts (again, second car first).
	4 Start the second car and let it run for a few minutes.
	5 Start your car.

CHANGING A TYRE: MOTORCYCLE

Two wheels, the open road and a good pair of riding boots: Motorcycles are machines for men. The only other thing that will boost your standing as a man among men, besides riding a motorcycle, is working on one.

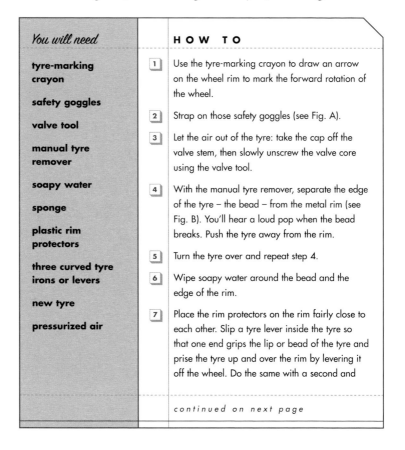

You will need	**H O W T O**
tyre-marking crayon	1. Use the tyre-marking crayon to draw an arrow on the wheel rim to mark the forward rotation of the wheel.
safety goggles	2. Strap on those safety goggles (see Fig. A).
valve tool	3. Let the air out of the tyre: take the cap off the valve stem, then slowly unscrew the valve core using the valve tool.
manual tyre remover	
soapy water	4. With the manual tyre remover, separate the edge of the tyre – the bead – from the metal rim (see Fig. B). You'll hear a loud pop when the bead breaks. Push the tyre away from the rim.
sponge	
plastic rim protectors	
three curved tyre irons or levers	5. Turn the tyre over and repeat step 4.
	6. Wipe soapy water around the bead and the edge of the rim.
new tyre	7. Place the rim protectors on the rim fairly close to each other. Slip a tyre lever inside the tyre so that one end grips the lip or bead of the tyre and prise the tyre up and over the rim by levering it off the wheel. Do the same with a second and
pressurized air	

continued on next page

continued

and third tyre lever while keeping the first one in place. With part of the tyre bead over the rim you should be able to pull the entire tyre off the wheel.

8   Line up the rotation arrow on the wheel with the rotation arrow on the new tyre (see Fig. C). Wipe the new tyre with soapy water and push one side of it onto the wheel rim with your hands.

9   Use your tyre levers and rim protectors to prise the rest of the new tyre on to the rim. This will take all three levers – two to keep the bead already on the rim in place and a third to work the rest of it down (see Fig. D).

10   Inflate the tyre so that its beads become seated in the ridges on the wheel rim – you'll hear a loud pop when this happens.

Fig. A

Fig. B

Fig. C

Fig. D

CHANGING A TYRE: BICYCLE

These pedal-powered machines can be as high tech as a Ducati motorbike, with rear suspension, front shocks and disc brakes, but are much easier to work on. If you ride a lot, there is one thing you need to know about: tyres. Fixing a flat bicycle tyre is easy and can save you a long, humiliating walk back to civilization and the bike shop.

You will need		**H O W T O**
tyre levers	1	Make sure all the air is out of the tyre and un-screw the round nut at the base of the valve stem.
new inner tube, if necessary	2	Starting opposite the valve stem, hook two tyre levers under the lip of the tyre and prise it over the rim. Work your way towards the valve stem.
hand pump		
tyre-marking crayon	3	Once you have one side of the tyre over the rim, remove the inner tube, poking the valve stem through the rim. Take care not to bend or pinch the valve stem, as this can cause a puncture in the tube near the stem and you'll have to install a new inner tube altogether.
patch kit with scraper, patch and glue		
	4	Connect the inner tube to a hand pump and pump it up as much as possible. Locate the puncture by listening for air around the tube. Once you find the hole, circle it with crayon.
	5	Scuff the inner tube with the metal scraper until the area on and around the puncture is rough. Spread the area with glue.

continued on next page

c o n t i n u e d

6 | When it dries, peel off the back of a patch and stick it firmly over the hole in the inner tube.

7 | Pump up the tube slightly and fit it back into the tyre that is still half on, half off the rim. Put the valve stem back through the hole in the rim.

8 | Force the tyre back into position on the rim, using tyre levers if need be.

9 | Screw the round nut back on to the valve stem, pump up the tyre and hit that trail again.

H I N T

✓ | Tyre levers can pinch a hole in an inner tube and flatten it all over again, so take care when removing and replacing the tyre.

CHAIN TROUBLES

Greasy, grimy bicycle chains get dirty very easily. If they get too dirty they won't catch the cogs on the rear wheel derailleur and the chain will skip whenever you shift gears. In order to keep the dirt and grease to a minimum, clean the chain regularly (say once a week) with a rag and some kind of grease solvent.

If your chain skips despite the weekly cleaning routine, it might be that there is a worn cog on the wheel (in which case the cog will need replacing) or there may be one or two links of your chain that are too tightly pinched together. If this is the case, turn the bike upside down and backpedal while looking for a tight link. You'll see it skip the cog. To loosen it, first try flexing it from side to side. If that doesn't work, or if the chain is rusted in several places, replace it all together.

MAN
ABOUT THE
HOUSE

When a window breaks or the sink leaks, when it's time to paint a room or lay down carpet, a man without tools is like a lion without claws. He is helpless. No longer the king of his domain, he will be forced to stand at a safe distance, peaking longingly into rooms or garages where other people do the work that he cannot do for himself. Don't let this happen to you: spare yourself the humiliation and get yourself equipped.

A MAN AND HIS TOOLS

Men have carried tools of some kind since time began and, in a way, owning the latest cordless electric drill or taking pleasure in the heft and balance of a good hammer is all part of our self-sustaining nature (in addition to providing most of our conversational repertoire). Compiling a complete set of tools may take time, but there are a few essentials for the beginner's toolbox. And remember: the better the quality, the longer a tool will last. Of course, you will need a workshop. This can be anything from a tight corner of the garage – sharing space with ugly lamps and stacks of do-it-yourself manuals – to an entire room dedicated to a lifetime of building projects.

You will need

claw hammer with a fibreglass shaft

nail punch

set of Phillips-head and flathead screwdrivers

25-ft/7.5-m steel tape measure

crosscut saw

hacksaw

slip-joint pliers

needle-nose pliers

adjustable wrench

torpedo level

Stanley knife

wood plane

set of chisels

plunger

3.5-amp variable-speed electric drill (corded or cordless)

set of drill bits

power saw

A P E R F E C T W O R K S H O P H A S :

☑ Space, ventilation and light.

☑ Large entrance with big sliding doors.

☑ Extra-tall ceilings and plenty of windows to let light in and dust out. (Built-in vacuum systems also help keep sawdust and fumes to a minimum.)

☑ A workbench, made from the finest hardwood and outfitted with built-in vices.

☑ Separate stations for cutting, fastening, painting and stripping.

☑ A table saw, a jointer and a band saw.

☑ Plenty of storage: shelving space as well as peg boards to help keep tools organized and within easy reach.

HOW TO TAKE SOMETHING APART
(AND PUT IT BACK TOGETHER AGAIN)

If you never read instructions for model aeroplane kits when you were a kid, chances are you'll find yourself in a heated panic after disassembling your car's rear brakes and realizing you have no idea how to put them back together. Do yourself a favour and devise a system for working properly.

You will need		**HOW TO**
clean, flat surface	1	Clear a large flat work surface to give yourself enough room to lay out each part – somewhere away from crazed pets and children.
masking tape		
pen	2	Label each part as you remove it by sticking on a piece of masking tape and assigning it a number. Place each part on the work surface in rows with masking tape (and numbers) visible.
paper		
	3	Write down the number and a description of the part. Note where you found it and how it fitted onto the assembly. It may help to draw a sketch of the piece in the direction it was pointing before you removed it.
	4	When it comes time to reassemble the parts, pick them up, starting with the last number, and work your way back to the beginning.

SHORT CUT

X	There are no short cuts. Go one piece at a time and don't rush.

APPLIANCE REPAIR

Machines always break, even the best ones. That's why a man has to know how to fix them.

WASHING MACHINE

Washing colours and whites separately is one thing. A washing machine that won't start or spin is another. If the repair involves the solenoid, spin clutch or transmission, call a professional. If the machine is just full of water, you can check the drainage system for those lost socks.

WHAT TO DO

1 First, see that the drainage hose isn't kinked, bent or blocked in a way that prevents water from passing.

2 Bail out as much water as you can.

3 Unhook the hose from the machine, remembering to plan for all the water that's going to spill out. Look for a sock, a handkerchief or anything that could clog the hose and remove it.

4 If the hose is clear, something could be clogging the pump, in which case refer to the owner's manual.

5 If the machine won't fill up with water, check for anything that might be clogging the fill hose. If that's clear and the hose isn't kinked, remove the hose to get at the screen filters inside the valves at the back of the machine.

6 Don't remove the cone-shaped screens, but do clean them of any fluff, dirt or grime.

VACUUM CLEANER

If the machine won't turn on, check the connection and make sure you haven't blown a fuse. It could be that the tiny engine is shot, in which case you should get it replaced. If the vacuum won't suck properly there are a few things you can do yourself.

WHAT TO DO

1. If the vacuum cleaner is old it may just need a couple of minor adjustments. If an electrical cord is frayed and not connecting properly, re-splice the wires together and patch the splice with plenty of electrical tape.

2. Check that the hose doesn't have any holes in it. If it does, wrap the hose and the holes with more electrical tape.

3. Change overstuffed dust bags or clogged filters (if your vacuum cleaner has them). They tend to inhibit the sucking mechanism of a vacuum.

4. Check that the round, spinning brush thing under the vacuum – technically an agitator – is, in fact, spinning. If not, the rubber belt attached to it may be broken or there might be hair or string wrapped around the agitator, preventing it from doing its job. String and hair around the agitator can also burn out an engine. Belts can be replaced by removing the bottom plate assembly with a screwdriver. Check the manufacturer's manual for details.

5. Some vacuum cleaners with agitators and brushes need to be adjusted so that they are an appropriate height off the carpet. Too close, and the sucking mechanism is effectively smothered.

6. For a vacuum cleaner with a tube, make sure there isn't anything clogging it.

TOASTER

Sticking a knife into a toaster is not a great way to start your day, especially if you discover a few thousand volts of electricity instead of a golden brown piece of bread. Before tossing the toaster out with the rubbish, however, try to find out what is wrong.

WHAT TO DO

[1] If toast won't pop up it could be that there are crumbs clogging the runners on the lift mechanism. Turn the toaster upside down over the sink and shake well.

[2] For a toaster whose heating element no longer glows, first make sure the toaster is plugged in correctly and that there is no damage to the cord. If the cord is fine, there may be a break in the toaster element.

[3] Unplug the toaster and, using a repair manual as a guide, turn the toaster upside down and remove the bottom plate with a screwdriver to access the heating element. If the element is damaged, repair it with special sleeves you can buy at a hardware store.

[4] If toast won't stay down you might have to replace the latch spring.

HINT

[✓] Old toasters, especially those from the 1950s, have long been considered collector's items because of their unique design. So, even if you can't get your old toaster fired up, you can probably clean it up with some chrome polish and a little oil and use it as a cool retro bookend or something.

BASIC PLUMBING

Plumbing is one of those jobs men fear. Nevertheless, being able to eradicate the plink, plink, plink of a dripping tap is a crucial bit of know-how and will help preserve both your own sanity and that of anyone living in the house with you.

FIXING A DRIPPING TAP

The most common kinds of tap are the old-fashioned two-handle hot and cold ones and the newer, single-handled cartridge taps.

You will need		HOW TO
screwdriver (flathead or Phillips, depending on the tap)	1	Turn off the main water valve – usually under the sink.
	2	In most cases, the cause of a dripping two-handled tap is the seat washer, which you can access through either handle.
adjustable wrench		
cloth	3	Determine if it's the hot or cold water that's dripping, then unscrew the top of the handle with a screwdriver (see Fig. A). If your tap has a decorative "bonnet" under the handle, use an adjustable wrench to remove it, covering the bonnet with a cloth to avoid scratching it.
new seat washer (for a two-handled tap)		
needle-nose pliers		
new cartridge (for a single-handled tap)	4	What you see now is the packing nut. Use an adjustable wrench to unscrew the nut and pull out the entire stem assembly from the handle (see Figs. B and C). At the base of the stem is the seat washer. Replace it and put the handle back together (see Fig. D).
		continued on next page

continued

5 For a single-handled cartridge tap, unscrew the handle and the bonnet and grab the cartridge with a pair of needle-nose pliers. Pull it straight up and out.

6 Replace the cartridge and put the assembly back together.

H I N T

☑ If your tap is not dripping but is leaking at the handle, it is more than likely that the O-ring gasket at the top of the stem or cartridge is worn out. To get to it, take off the handle and bonnet. The O-ring will be around the stem, just under the packing nut, and is easy to replace.

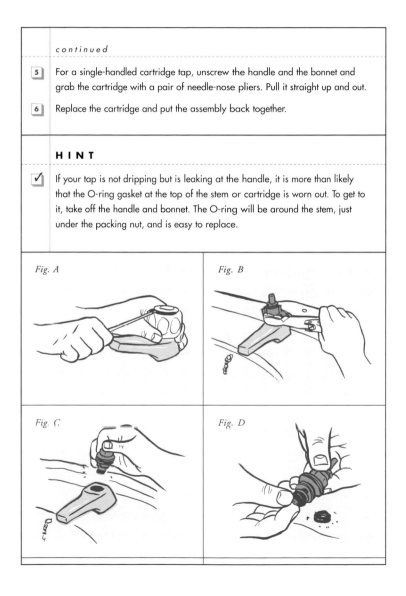

Fig. A

Fig. B

Fig. C

Fig. D

UNBLOCKING A SINK

A sink filled with murky water will not impress a lady (if you're lucky enough to get one over to your house). It's gross and it doesn't have to be that way.

You will need	**HOW TO**
cloth	**1** If a sink is clogged, try unclogging it with a plunger. First, stuff a wet cloth into the overflow drain so that the plunger will have maximum suction. Run a little water into the sink (1-2in/ 3-5cm). Plunge away, making sure you get a nice flat connection to the sink.
plunger	
liquid chemical cleaner	
auger	**2** If that doesn't work, pour a liquid chemical cleaner into the drain, following manufacturer's instructions.
screwdriver	
adjustable wrench	**3** If the sink is still blocked, use a plumbing auger to clean it. Push the auger into the drain. As it goes in, rotate it until it breaks through or dislodges the debris.
	4 Another way to unblock a sink is to unscrew and clean out the trap. Place a pan under the trap and use an adjustable wrench to remove the clean-out plug. If there's no clean-out plug, remove the whole trap.

HINT

✓ It's always a good idea to keep a plumber's phone number nearby in case of an emergency. You never know when you'll wake up to burst pipes, exploding hot-water heaters or overflowing kitchen disposals.

BASIC ELECTRICS

Working with electricity is not always trouble-free, but you can eliminate the more dangerous problems by turning off the main power before you start.

REPLACING A BLOWN FUSE

Circuit breakers or fuses serve as safety valves for the house: if a circuit overloads, then its fuse or circuit breaker will be triggered and the electricity cut off. Resetting a circuit breaker is as easy as flipping the switch, while a blown fuse has to be replaced. This, itself, is an easy fix. And since nobody else wants to work with electricity because it is dangerous, this is a job that will much improve your standing in the house.

You will need		**HOW TO**
new fuse	1	Turn off the power at the fuse box by pulling out the main disconnect panel.
	2	Screw out the blown fuse in an anticlockwise direction. If the fuse is a cartridge, pull it straight out.
	3	Replace the blown fuse with one of the same capacity.
	4	Replace the main disconnect panel to return power to the house.

HINT	
X	Never stand in water when dealing with electricity.

REWIRING A LAMP AND ADDING A NEW PLUG

If a lamp flickers all the time, or won't turn, it might be that the cord is frayed or cracked. If so, it won't hurt to replace the wiring.

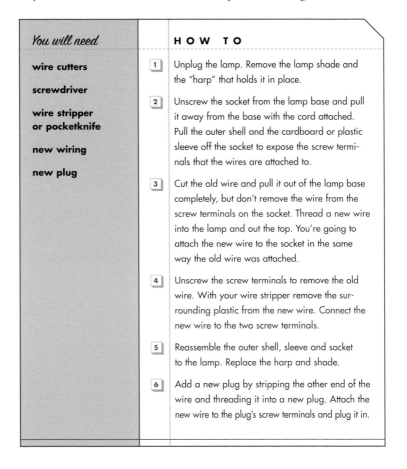

You will need

wire cutters

screwdriver

wire stripper or pocketknife

new wiring

new plug

H O W   T O

1. Unplug the lamp. Remove the lamp shade and the "harp" that holds it in place.

2. Unscrew the socket from the lamp base and pull it away from the base with the cord attached. Pull the outer shell and the cardboard or plastic sleeve off the socket to expose the screw terminals that the wires are attached to.

3. Cut the old wire and pull it out of the lamp base completely, but don't remove the wire from the screw terminals on the socket. Thread a new wire into the lamp and out the top. You're going to attach the new wire to the socket in the same way the old wire was attached.

4. Unscrew the screw terminals to remove the old wire. With your wire stripper remove the surrounding plastic from the new wire. Connect the new wire to the two screw terminals.

5. Reassemble the outer shell, sleeve and socket to the lamp. Replace the harp and shade.

6. Add a new plug by stripping the other end of the wire and threading it into a new plug. Attach the new wire to the plug's screw terminals and plug it in.

DRILLING THE PERFECT HOLE

While a steady hand will give you a good hole, it's the drill and the drill bit that do all the work. Drills come corded or cordless (for those hard-to-reach spots) and can be powered anywhere from just over 6 volts for light uses up to almost 18 for the really heavy-duty drilling jobs. A variable-speed, 9.6-volt drill – one that can rotate as slow as you want or go up to 1200 revolutions per minute – is all a man needs for the everyday household DIY project.

THE RIGHT BIT: To get the perfect hole, you'll need to choose the right bit. A simple auger bit may do a quick job on a 2x4 stud but it's not the best thing to use on stone, brick, metal, glass or even a nice piece of mahogany trim. Spade bits cut clean, wide holes in wood while carbide-tipped masonry bits should be used for concrete, stone or brick. A twist bit can cut neat, but small, holes through metal or wood. Drill faster for metal and slow it down for wood. Hole saws are used if you want to install a door knob or any other large round thing. If you're planning on drilling into easily breakable materials, glass or tile for example, you'll need a diamond-tipped drill bit.

TECHNIQUE: Once you get the right bit for the job, then it's all about technique. Hold the drill at a 90 degree angle and be sure to exert enough pressure on the drill as you go. The best way to do this is to use one hand to hold the drill handle and the other to push on the back of the drill right over where the bit is going into the hole. If you need to drill to a specific depth (rather than all the way through something) there are collars and drill stops to get you what you want. Also, make sure the drill bit is sharp and not too nicked. A dull or damaged bit could cause the wood to splinter at the exit hole.

FLOORING

Laying vinyl tiles, carpet or wood flooring is not that hard to do. Some adhesive here, a staple or a nail there, is all it takes to have a sharp new floor – impressive skills for the man about the house.

VINYL FLOOR

You'll be glad to know that vinyl tiles don't look like they used to back in the 70s. There's actually some good-looking and durable stuff out there.

You will need	**HOW TO**
hammer	1 Using a hammer and a nail punch, sink any existing nails or screw heads into the floor. The plywood subfloor should be as smooth and flat as possible.
nail punch	
chalk line	
tile adhesive	2 Snap two chalk lines across the room so that they meet in the centre at 90-degree angles and divide the room into four equal quadrants.
notched trowel	
vinyl tiles	3 Starting in the middle, use a notched trowel and spread enough adhesive in one quadrant to support four tiles at a time.
Stanley knife	
	4 Working from the centre out to the walls, lay four tiles in the first quadrant, then in the next three before returning to the first quadrant and so on until the floor is covered.

TIP

☑ To cut a tile use a straight edge as a guide and make several passes with a Stanley knife until it cuts all the way through.

CARPET

Carpet can be installed in a room in several different ways. This method uses strips of wood, which are filled with upward-pointing tacks.

You will need		HOW TO
hammer	1	Remove all furniture and make sure the floor is clean. Nail down the tackless strips around the room about 1/2in/1cm from every wall. If you have a concrete floor, use masonry nails or a strong adhesive to secure the strips to the floor.
nails		
tackless strips		
masonry nails or adhesive (if you have a concrete floor)	2	Trim the underlay to fit the area inside tackless strips. Staple or adhere it to the floor.
	3	Roll out the carpet over the underlay and the tackless strips so that it fits roughly in the room. Trim away the excess, taking care to leave 1–2in/3–5cm extra carpet all around.
sharp carpet knife		
scissors (big enough to cut carpet)		
knee kicker	4	Attach the carpet to the tackless strips along one wall using the knee kicker. Trim any excess to fit, and use a putty knife to tuck the edge of the carpet under the skirting.
underlay		
carpet	5	Do all of one wall first, then repeat the process on the opposite wall. Make sure you pull the carpet tight so that there are no loose spots in the middle of the room. When that's done, take care of the other two walls in the same manner.

HINT

✓ To determine how much carpet to order for any given room, measure the room at its longest and widest points and multiply. That gives you the area in square feet/metres. (To get square yardage, divide the square footage by nine.)

WOOD FLOORS

Once bypassed for the luxury of a shag carpet, wood floors are solid, natural and age well – all qualities that every real man should aspire to.

You will need		**H O W T O**
tongue-and-groove hardwood flooring	1	Remove any skirting and beading in the room where the wood floor is going down.
chalk line	2	To avoid having two seams line up next to each other, make sure you alternate the lengths of wood. Measure, cut and fit the strips together on the floor of the room in a dry run before you start nailing. Plan for a $1/4$-in/$1/2$-cm gap around the entire room between the wall and the wood floor to allow for the skirting boards.
hammer		
1 $1/2$in/3$1/2$cm finish nails		
nail punch		
small crowbar	3	For the first strip, use as long a board as you have and snap a chalk line on the floor to use as a guide for the first strip. Be sure to leave the $1/4$-in/$1/2$-cm gap.
pneumatic floor nailer		
table saw	4	Taking care to align the wood with the chalk line, drive a nail every 12in/30cm into the face of the first strip. To avoid damaging the wood, stop hammering when you get close, and use a nail punch to drive the nail below the surface.
	5	Next start piecing the other strips together on the floor. Fit the tongues into the grooves tightly and use the pneumatic nailer and a mallet to drive staples every 12in/30cm through the tongue of each length of board.

continued on next page

continued

6   When you get to the last strip, use a small crowbar to ease the board into the last course and face-nail it to the subfloor as in step 4.

7   Sand the floor with a heavy-duty disc sander. Then stain and brush on several coats of high-gloss polyurethane finish. Replace beading to cover any gaps at the edges.

T I P

✓   When fitting the tongue-and-groove boards together you may need to hammer them into place to get a snug fit. Instead of hammering straight onto the tongue of a board and risk breaking it, use a scrap of flooring as a buffer to your hammer

WALLPAPERING

Contrary to current popular thinking, hanging wallpaper is not for wimps. Let's face it, manhandling several yards of glue-filled paper, plus sponge, spreader and Stanley knife up a stepladder is no picnic (especially when you find you've left the sponge at the bottom). On the other hand, anything that has the potential of making a big sticky mess is real work and deserves to be added to every handyman's repertoire.

Using your mum's dining-room table is not in your best interests, so why not make a workbench. Simply top two sawhorses with a 4x6-ft/1.5x2-m piece of $3/4$-in/2-cm thick plywood and, voila! – instant table.

You will need		**HOW TO**
tape measure	1	Calculate the number of rolls of paper you need by measuring the surface area of the wall to be covered and divide by 56 (the coverage of a typical metric roll).
Stanley knife		
plumb		
pencil	2	Measure the height of the wall to be covered and cut strips 2in/5cm longer than needed for extra slack. This is the easiest part of the job and, therefore, the best time to impress people.
straight edge or spirit level		
flat surface or table	3	Go to the middle of your wall and hang the plumb from the ceiling. Draw a line where it comes to rest; this is your guide for the first strip of wallpaper.
paintbrush		
paper smoother		
glue	4	Tape over light switches and plug sockets so they don't get any glue on them.
sponge		
		continued on next page

continued

5   Don't hold back with the glue. Slap it on to each strip of paper with a paint-brush and "book" the strip by folding it loosely into a concertina. Glue may squirt out at the sides. There is no need to panic.

6   Take the booked strip to the wall and, starting at the top, unfold it along the plumb line you drew earlier, smoothing it on to the wall as you go. Keep your cool and slide the strip into place, taking care not to stretch the paper.

7   Next, use a smoother to get out any bubbles and get the paper snug into the corner of the wall and the floor. Wipe off any excess glue with a wet sponge and cut off the overlap with a Stanley knife.

8   Continue this process around the room. Each time you come to a window, light switch or plug cover paste and smooth the strip to the wall before cutting. When you get to a corner, it's OK for the strip to carry over on to the adjoining wall. Just start the next piece right in the corner, overlapping the excess.

PAINTING A ROOM

This sounds easy, and it is, but you have to prepare the room thoroughly first. Check all wooden surfaces for nails. Sink any below the surface with a hammer and nail punch and fill with wood filler. For small holes or cracks in the plaster, push Polyfilla into the damaged area while smoothing it out to the level of the surrounding wall. Use wood filler to fill in gaps along skirtings, architraves and dado rails.

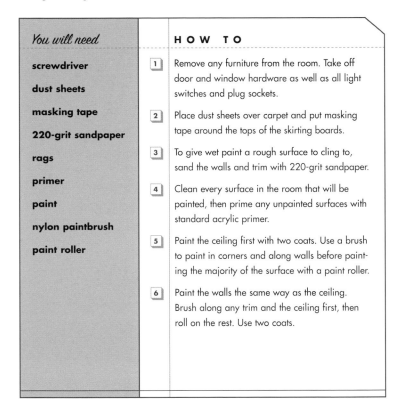

You will need

screwdriver

dust sheets

masking tape

220-grit sandpaper

rags

primer

paint

nylon paintbrush

paint roller

HOW TO

1. Remove any furniture from the room. Take off door and window hardware as well as all light switches and plug sockets.

2. Place dust sheets over carpet and put masking tape around the tops of the skirting boards.

3. To give wet paint a rough surface to cling to, sand the walls and trim with 220-grit sandpaper.

4. Clean every surface in the room that will be painted, then prime any unpainted surfaces with standard acrylic primer.

5. Paint the ceiling first with two coats. Use a brush to paint in corners and along walls before painting the majority of the surface with a paint roller.

6. Paint the walls the same way as the ceiling. Brush along any trim and the ceiling first, then roll on the rest. Use two coats.

REPAIRING LARGE HOLES IN PLASTERBOARD

If you happen to trip over your paint bucket, accidentally ramming your head through the plaster, you can repair the hole you make with a patch.

You will need		HOW TO
pencil	1	Use a pencil and a square scrap of plasterboard (your front patch) to draw a square around the hole. Cut along the pencil line with the saw.
two scrap pieces of plasterboard	2	Now cut a second scrap of plasterboard 1in/2.5cm bigger on all sides than the first one. This is the back patch. Drill a finger hole in the middle of it and apply adhesive to its edges.
plasterboard saw		
plasterboard adhesive		
putty knife and Polyfilla	3	Tilt the back patch into the hole and flip it flush against the inside of the wall so that it covers the square hole. Use the finger hole to hold it in place until the adhesive dries.
	4	Smear adhesive onto one side of your first patch. Fit it into the hole and against the back patch.
	5	Hide the newly patched hole by spreading Polyfilla over the joins. When that dries, sand the area down to make it even with the surrounding wall.

BUILDING A BOOKCASE

Shelving can be anything from a simple bracket job to a complex carpentry exercise, complete with dados and mortises. For sturdy, freestanding storage or bookshelves, one easy solution is to use cleats – small pieces of wood upon which the shelving boards can rest.

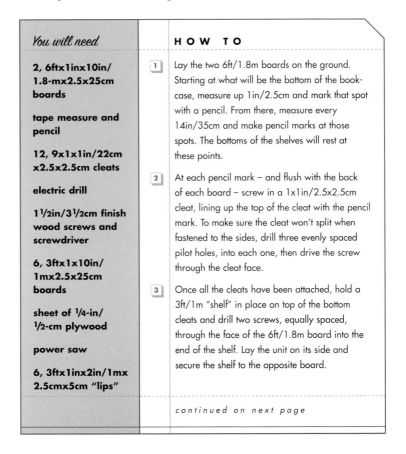

You will need

2, 6ftx1inx10in/ 1.8-mx2.5x25cm boards

tape measure and pencil

12, 9x1x1in/22cm x2.5x2.5cm cleats

electric drill

1 1/2in/3 1/2cm finish wood screws and screwdriver

6, 3ftx1x10in/ 1mx2.5x25cm boards

sheet of 1/4-in/ 1/2-cm plywood

power saw

6, 3ftx1inx2in/1mx 2.5cmx5cm "lips"

HOW TO

1. Lay the two 6ft/1.8m boards on the ground. Starting at what will be the bottom of the bookcase, measure up 1in/2.5cm and mark that spot with a pencil. From there, measure every 14in/35cm and make pencil marks at those spots. The bottoms of the shelves will rest at these points.

2. At each pencil mark – and flush with the back of each board – screw in a 1x1in/2.5x2.5cm cleat, lining up the top of the cleat with the pencil mark. To make sure the cleat won't split when fastened to the sides, drill three evenly spaced pilot holes, into each one, then drive the screw through the cleat face.

3. Once all the cleats have been attached, hold a 3ft/1m "shelf" in place on top of the bottom cleats and drill two screws, equally spaced, through the face of the 6ft/1.8m board into the end of the shelf. Lay the unit on its side and secure the shelf to the opposite board.

continued on next page

continued

4   Leave the unit lying on its side and secure the top shelf, then the rest of the shelves.

5   Measure and cut the sheet of plywood to fit on the back of the shelving unit. Fasten it with screws, spaced every 10in/25cm around its perimeter.

6   To finish the project, attach the "lips" to the front of the unit, under each shelf. Make sure they are flush with the bottom of the shelves and drive one screw into each end through the outer face of the bookshelf sides.

THE
PERFECT
HOST

Whether eating à deux or with friends and family, ordering in Chinese food or popping out to the corner bistro, it's important to be a good host. That means brushing up on your manners and creating an easy atmosphere with a little know-how and a take-charge attitude.

PLAYING HOST

As the host of a party, it's up to you to make sure the evening goes off without a hitch. Putting out drinks and food and getting a bunch of friends together is one thing. Keeping the conversation lively, the music great and the glasses and dinner plates full is another.

THE HOUSE PARTY

House parties tend to take on lives of their own and all you have to do is guide the chaos, at least until midnight. What makes unpredictable evenings so smooth and fun is the work you do ahead of time. Before anyone shows up, make sure you get the fridge fully stocked with drinks, and order your keg. For food, place inviting bowls of snacks strategically around the house.

As soon as guests arrive offer to take their coats and give them a drink – a simple enough task. Things get tricky, however, when you start having to remember names, and it's always impressive to know a little something about each guest. That way you can offer nuggets of information when you introduce people who don't know each other. "Alan Greene this is Jane Barclay," you might say. "She just got back from the coast. Alan is an avid fisherman." That should be enough to get them going and you can peel off to work the rest of the room.

On the flip side it's also your job to keep certain guests apart. If you see a friend cornered by someone who won't stop talking, you have to get in there and break up the logjam. And don't just let quiet folk wander around aimlessly. Bring them into the fold and make sure they're having fun. In the meantime, enjoy yourself. There's nothing worse than a host who won't get over the fact that the caterers set the dining-room table on fire. Besides, it's not a party until something gets broken. (When else are you going to use that perfect workshop?)

THE DINNER PARTY

Hosting a dinner party for a group of friends takes a good deal of planning and quite a lot can go wrong. The good thing is that it is not as intimate as a romantic dinner for two, so it's okay if events get the better of you. For guaranteed success, make sure you invite one or two guests that can keep a rapt house whatever happens.

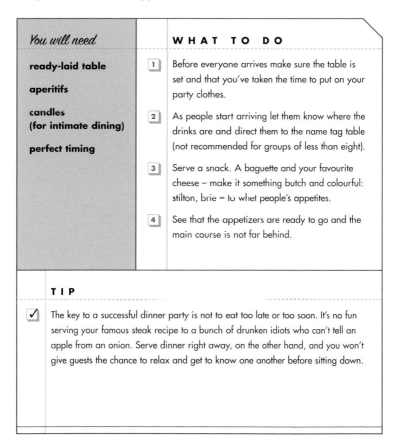

You will need

ready-laid table

aperitifs

**candles
(for intimate dining)**

perfect timing

WHAT TO DO

1. Before everyone arrives make sure the table is set and that you've taken the time to put on your party clothes.

2. As people start arriving let them know where the drinks are and direct them to the name tag table (not recommended for groups of less than eight).

3. Serve a snack. A baguette and your favourite cheese – make it something butch and colourful: stilton, brie – to whet people's appetites.

4. See that the appetizers are ready to go and the main course is not far behind.

TIP

✓ The key to a successful dinner party is not to eat too late or too soon. It's no fun serving your famous steak recipe to a bunch of drunken idiots who can't tell an apple from an onion. Serve dinner right away, on the other hand, and you won't give guests the chance to relax and get to know one another before sitting down.

HOW TO CARVE A ROAST

Carving a roast takes a sharp knife, a little know-how and a fair bit of courage. Not only do you have to stand at the head of the table slicing the evening meal into palatable portions, you also have to look good doing it (taking your shirt off is not an option here). This is man's work, to be sure.

You will need	CARVING A RIB ROAST
large fork	1 Stand the roast on its end so the ribs are facing to the left.
10-in/25-cm, extra-sharp carving knife	2 Keeping your knife close to the bone, make a small downward cut along the ribs.
	3 Cut thin slices horizontally towards the ribs (and the cut).
	4 Repeat this process until all the meat is sliced.

CARVING A TURKEY

1 Make sure the plate is turned so that the bird's legs are pointing to your right (see Fig. A).

2 Using a fork to steady the beast, cut down between the leg and the breast, carefully finding the thigh joint. Cut off the leg and thigh through the joint (see Fig. B). Repeat for the other leg. Cut the leg from the thigh on a separate plate.

3 Now cut off the wings. By slicing down between the wing and the breast, you should also be able to find a joint here that will make removing the wings easier (see Fig. C).

continued on next page

continued

4 Cutting the breast is next. Slice from the outside in towards the breastbone in long thin pieces (see Fig. D). Then turn the plate around and repeat the process on the other side.

H I N T

☑ Be sure to let your roast sit for five to ten minutes before carving. During cooking, all the juices concentrate in the middle of the meat, away from the heat. Letting the meat stand will give the juices a chance to relax again, making the roast easier to carve.

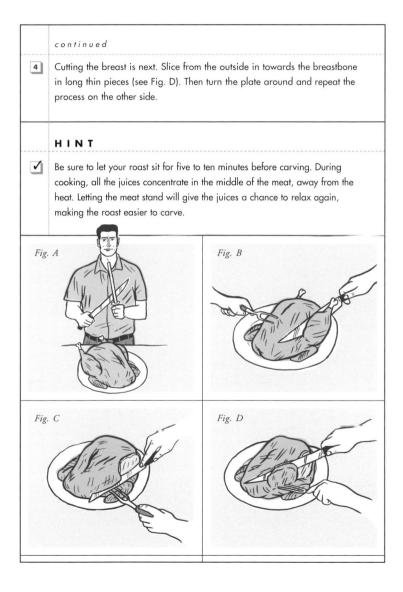

Fig. A

Fig. B

Fig. C

Fig. D

WHAT TO DRINK AND WHEN

Choosing the right drink for the right occasion is something a man should know about. Although there are no strict rules about how or when to serve alcohol (because you can always think of a reason to booze things up), you'll score extra points for serving a drink in the right glass.

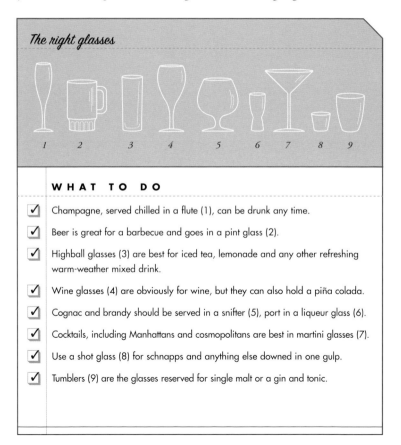

The right glasses

1   2   3   4   5   6   7   8   9

WHAT TO DO

☑ Champagne, served chilled in a flute (1), can be drunk any time.

☑ Beer is great for a barbecue and goes in a pint glass (2).

☑ Highball glasses (3) are best for iced tea, lemonade and any other refreshing warm-weather mixed drink.

☑ Wine glasses (4) are obviously for wine, but they can also hold a piña colada.

☑ Cognac and brandy should be served in a snifter (5), port in a liqueur glass (6).

☑ Cocktails, including Manhattans and cosmopolitans are best in martini glasses (7).

☑ Use a shot glass (8) for schnapps and anything else downed in one gulp.

☑ Tumblers (9) are the glasses reserved for single malt or a gin and tonic.

STORING WINE

Digging out a basement for a good wine cellar would be at the top of any man's to-do list if it weren't for the fact that he'd have to sell the house to afford it. That doesn't mean we all can't keep a few bottles of wine on hand. Just be sure to follow a few storing tips when you do.

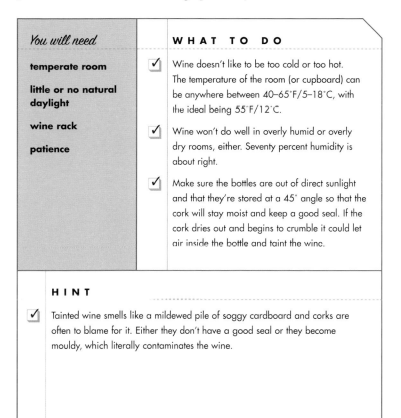

You will need

temperate room

little or no natural daylight

wine rack

patience

W H A T   T O   D O

✓ Wine doesn't like to be too cold or too hot. The temperature of the room (or cupboard) can be anywhere between 40–65°F/5–18°C, with the ideal being 55°F/12°C.

✓ Wine won't do well in overly humid or overly dry rooms, either. Seventy percent humidity is about right.

✓ Make sure the bottles are out of direct sunlight and that they're stored at a 45° angle so that the cork will stay moist and keep a good seal. If the cork dries out and begins to crumble it could let air inside the bottle and taint the wine.

H I N T

✓ Tainted wine smells like a mildewed pile of soggy cardboard and corks are often to blame for it. Either they don't have a good seal or they become mouldy, which literally contaminates the wine.

MIXING THE PERFECT COCKTAIL

Apparently there are a hundred ways to make a gin martini – a drink with only two ingredients, excluding the olives. The best way is to pour the gin over ice (where it is stirred, not shaken lest the gin bruise) before removing the vermouth from the shelf. The next step is to strain the gin into the glass, drop in two olives and serve the drink, all while thinking about – but not touching – the vermouth. That is enough to make the perfect martini.

It takes practice to come up with a winner like that but most good cocktails have a few standard ingredients. Here are a few perfect takes on some old standbys.

POPE PAUL'S BLOODY MARY MIX

This heavenly cocktail is a Saturday morning saviour after a night in the pub, watching the game and hoovering beer like there's no tomorrow.

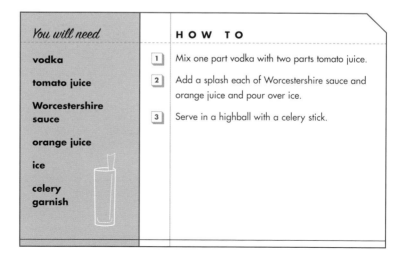

You will need	HOW TO
vodka	**1** Mix one part vodka with two parts tomato juice.
tomato juice	**2** Add a splash each of Worcestershire sauce and orange juice and pour over ice.
Worcestershire sauce	**3** Serve in a highball with a celery stick.
orange juice	
ice	
celery garnish	

A BOY NAMED SUE'S
MAN-IN-BLACK MARGARITAS

If you haven't actually turned into Johnny Cash after three of these babies, you will certainly think you have.

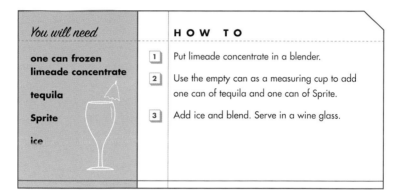

You will need		HOW TO
one can frozen limeade concentrate	1	Put limeade concentrate in a blender.
tequila	2	Use the empty can as a measuring cup to add one can of tequila and one can of Sprite.
Sprite	3	Add ice and blend. Serve in a wine glass.
ice		

SLIM'S GIN AND GINGER

You can drink this as you watch the evening summer rainfall from your front porch. (A real man should have his sensitive, contemplative side.)

You will need		HOW TO
gin	1	Mix one part gin and one part ginger ale over ice.
ginger ale	2	Stir and garnish with a wedge of lime.
ice	3	Serve in a martini glass at croquet tournaments or other lawn parties.
lime		

WHEN AND HOW
TO PROPOSE A TOAST

Lifting a glass and offering a toast is a lost art in need of a revival. In the past men would quieten huge crowds – or inspire small ones – with a glass of champagne, a few well-placed words and a verbal nod to the guest of honour. Today's equivalent is a loud *Salud!* at the pub with your mates. Still, a toast will always be a welcome show and the host who steps onto a chair to give one can call the party a success no matter what else happens.

You will need	**HOW TO**
glass, half full (preferably with champagne, but anything will do)	1. When the time comes, make sure everyone has a drink to toast with.
	2. Get everyone's attention (clinking a glass with a fork is the convention; shouting "Oi!" isn't).
idea of what you want to say	3. Hold your right arm and glass straight out in front of you. Be sure and look the recipient of your words in the eye.
the guts to say it	4. When it's time to touch glasses with everyone in the room, look each person in the eye as you toast them with your glass.

DO'S AND DON'TS

✓ Do think carefully about what you want to say long before any guests arrive at your house, and have the first few lines written down in case of stage fright.

✗ Don't go on for too long. Your toast might turn into a sermon and people will start looking around for more booze.

CLEANING UP

Now that the party's over, it's time to put your house back together.

H O W   T O

1. Take care of leftover food before going off to bed. If you're left with plates and cookware, bag up the scraps and at least soak the dishes.

2. Crank open the windows and doors to get the air circulating.

3. Collect all cups, bottles and cans. Empty ashtrays into bin bags.

4. Swab out the bathroom.

5. Sweep the floors well, then fire up the mop bucket. The trouble areas will be those where your shoes stick most.

6. If you have carpet, hire a steam cleaner and shampoo the hell out of it.

GAINING POINTS
WITH THE
FAIRER SEX

First impressions are important. If you think James Dean never made the effort to comb his coif or look his best at any time of the day or night, then you're mistaken. Like most men, he knew that if you're looking to gain some ground with the ladies, the first thing you have to do is look good. Most people can tell if they're going to like or dislike you almost instantly, so appearance is important and how you act is crucial.

HOW TO IRON A SHIRT

It is a fact of life that wearing a wrinkled shirt looks bad. Not only will no one listen to you during meetings at work, but if you show up on a date looking like you just rolled out of bed, don't be surprised if you're alone in the bar by 9 p.m. There are two solutions to this problem. One is to take all your shirts to the cleaners, which is a good idea, if an expensive one. The other is to iron the shirts yourself.

You will need	**H O W T O**
new iron **distilled water (for steam)** **ironing board**	**1** Be sure to set the iron temperature to the correct setting (irons usually have settings based on the type of material you're ironing). Linen shirts can get singed and will turn brown in places if the iron is too hot. Then you have a bigger problem than wrinkles.
	2 Spread the shirt flat on the ironing board and press the back of the collar first (see Fig. A).
	3 Flip it over and press the front of the collar. Be sure to iron from the ends towards the centre as collars tend to crease.
	4 Next iron the cuffs. Open them up and do the insides first and then the outsides (see Fig. B).
	5 Iron the sleeves. Lay them flat on the board and smooth them out so you don't press any creases into the material. Iron in slow deliberate movements, smoothing and straightening as you go.
	continued on next page

continued

6. To iron the shoulders, fit the armholes on the end of the board (see Fig. C).

7. Iron the body of the shirt last. Lay the shirt so that the collar points towards the narrow end of the board and with one front side of the shirt flat on the board. Iron from the shoulder to the shirttails.

8. Rotate the shirt. Iron the back next and then the remaining front side (see Fig. D).

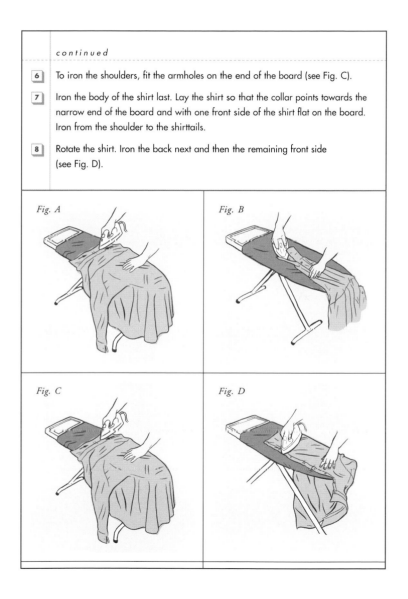

Fig. A

Fig. B

Fig. C

Fig. D

HOW TO SHAVE

The best thing you can do to get yourself cleaned up for a big date is to have a shower and shave. Even if you shaved earlier in the day, go ahead and take off that prickly five o'clock shadow. That way, if you spend the night dancing cheek to cheek with a woman, you won't give your date's face a bad case of carpet burn. There's nothing sexy about kissing what amounts to a sheet of sandpaper.

You will need		**H O W T O**
hot water	1	Wash your face with hot water and facial soap.
facial soap	2	Get a small towel wet with hot water (as hot as you can stand it) and use as a hot pack on your face for about two minutes. The water and the heat help soften tough facial hair.
small towel		
shaving soap		
shaving mug	3	Mix up a batch of shaving soap in your shaving mug.
shaving brush	4	Run hot water over the shaving brush before using it. Then apply the shaving soap to your face with the brush in small circular motions until you get a good foamy lather. The brush will help facial hair stand up.
new razor		
mirror		
	5	Shave the sideburns first to allow the soap to soak into your chin and upper lip (the tougher areas of a beard). Do not shave upwards or against the growth of the hair. When the sideburns are done, shave the cheeks, then the sides of the neck,
		continued on next page

continued on next page

continued

the neck, the upper lip, the lower lip and finally the chin. Rinse the razor after each pass.

6 Rinse your face with cold water, and apply an alcohol-based aftershave astringent or lotion to keep your face from getting irritated.

DO'S AND DON'TS

✗ Don't shave against the growth of your facial hair. It will irritate the skin.

✗ Don't slather on an alcohol-based aftershave if you have cut yourself.

✓ Do change razors every week. Using a dull razor increases your chance of cutting yourself.

✓ Do put tiny bits of tissue paper on any cuts you happen to inflict upon yourself. It will help the blood clot faster and it won't drip onto your white shirt collar.

LEARN HOW TO DANCE

Women love a man with good rhythm. No question about it, a man who can dance is a man who can charm the ladies. If you can organize a dinner with dancing afterwards, you're telling a woman that you have more to offer than your (albeit impressive) knowledge of good wine. You're telling her that you can be smooth and sophisticated as well as smart.

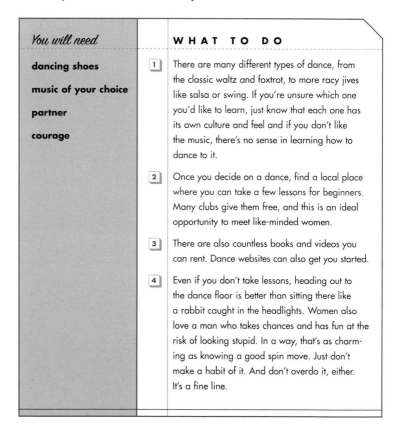

You will need	**WHAT TO DO**
dancing shoes **music of your choice** **partner** **courage**	**1** There are many different types of dance, from the classic waltz and foxtrot, to more racy jives like salsa or swing. If you're unsure which one you'd like to learn, just know that each one has its own culture and feel and if you don't like the music, there's no sense in learning how to dance to it.
	2 Once you decide on a dance, find a local place where you can take a few lessons for beginners. Many clubs give them free, and this is an ideal opportunity to meet like-minded women.
	3 There are also countless books and videos you can rent. Dance websites can also get you started.
	4 Even if you don't take lessons, heading out to the dance floor is better than sitting there like a rabbit caught in the headlights. Women also love a man who takes chances and has fun at the risk of looking stupid. In a way, that's as charming as knowing a good spin move. Just don't make a habit of it. And don't overdo it, either. It's a fine line.

THE FIRST DATE

Asking a woman out on a first date can be a little tricky. You want to be cool but not too cool, charming but not so much that you come off like an oleaginous playboy. What you don't want to do is drink a few martinis before you approach her because, instead of calming your nerves, booze will only make you look and smell drunk. It may have worked for Dean Martin, but he was rich and famous… sort of. So just stay confident and ask the girl if she wants to have dinner sometime. It's a casual approach, but your interest in her is clear. If she says yes, there are a few things that will guarantee your first date isn't also your last.

WHAT TO DO

- ✓ Keep the nose and ear hairs tamed. Bushy nose hair might be part of the culture in some parts of the world, but I guarantee you those men aren't getting any dates.

- ✓ Make sure your teeth are free of debris, and remember, bad breath is bad.

- ✓ Dousing yourself with Old Spice is not the same thing as having a shower. Take a normal bath and go easy on the cologne, if you use any at all.

- ✓ One-day beard growth can look cool, but three days just looks lazy.

- ✓ A new shirt will not only look good but it'll make you feel good.

- ✓ Pay attention to detail. A belt, clean socks and a clean handkerchief are essentials.

- ✓ Don't light up a smoke five minutes after meeting your date. In fact, don't smoke at all unless she smokes first.

- ✓ Don't be miserable. If you're gloomy and unhappy, why are you out on a date in the first place?

REMEMBERING DATES

Birthdays and anniversaries are important dates. Don't forget them. A lot of men do and it lands them in the doghouse for at least a year, at which time they get the chance to prove themselves all over again simply by remembering those dates. If you have trouble with important dates, take comfort in the fact that you are not alone. Then do something about it.

You will need		**H O W T O**
calendar(s)	1	Get a calendar (or two or three) and write in the dates for these momentous occasions.
notepaper	2	When the month that the date is in rolls around, write a note to yourself and tape it to your computer. If it falls off, tape it on again until after the day has passed.
tape		
palmtop computer		
organized friend	3	If you have a Palm Pilot, enter the dates and programme an alarm to go off the week before. Then programme it to sound again two days before, one day before and on the day of whatever it is you're celebrating.
	4	Have a better-organized friend call and remind you when the date arrives.

T I P

☑ Unfortunately, remembering just the big dates is not always enough. Some women want you to remember when you went on your first date or the day you left your job in the big city to move to the country. Make sure you know which dates are important to her so you're not caught short when one crops up.

THE PERFECT GIFT

Choosing a present for a woman has reduced many a man to a crushed and gibbering heap of indecision. Will it be too big? Will she like the colour? Is it the right size, the right cut, the right style? These are the questions that can turn a short trip to the shops into an odyssey, especially if you're shopping for a specific occasion like a birthday or an anniversary.

WHAT TO DO

- [✓] Surprising a woman with a ring can make quite an impact – perhaps more so if you've only been dating for a week or two. This present is usually reserved for wedding proposals. If you're already married, a ring on your anniversary can be a beautiful reminder.

- [✓] Giving a woman a new power drill for her birthday could be considered by some to have an ulterior motive behind it. Better stick to perfume or poetry.

- [✓] A gift of flowers on any day of the week is always a winner.

- [✓] A day at a spa, a full-body massage or a pedicure are all excellent gifts for birthdays and promotions at work.

- [✓] Gift certificates to a favourite shop can be good, but only once in a while. If she gets one for the anniversary, her birthday and Christmas, you may find your powers of imagination called into question.

HINT

- [✓] If you wake up one morning only to realize it's that special someone's birthday and you forgot to buy her a present, it's time to go into emergency mode. First, remain calm. Tell her you can't wait to give her the present you got for her, but that she'll have to wait until that afternoon. Then figure out what you're going to do.

OLD-FASHIONED GALLANTRY

Though there is no longer a need to cover puddles in the way that Sir Walter Raleigh did for Queen Elizabeth I in 1581, there are still a few forms of old-fashioned gallantry a man can use.

WHAT TO DO

- ✓ If it starts to rain, take off your coat and hold it over her head while you make a break for the nearest shelter.

- ✓ Hold doors open and let a woman walk ahead of you.

- ✓ Give a lady your seat on a crowded bus or tube.

- ✓ Stand up when a lady leaves a table and again when she returns.

- ✓ To keep her from getting muddied by passing cars, always walk on the outside of the pavement.

WHAT TO DO IF SHE FAINTS

In 1950s' movies, villains, monsters, playboys and other rogue characters – dead or alive – were able to play on a woman's emotions, making her grow light-headed so that she'd faint elegantly into the arms of her leading man. These days women collapse to the floor because they skip a meal or don't drink enough water at the dance club. If you're lucky enough to catch a fainting femme mid fall, you can count on at least a dinner date once you've revived her.

You will need		**WHAT TO DO**
fainted woman	1	Call a doctor.
pillow	2	Elevate the fallen woman's legs with a pillow. (A folded suit jacket or tablecloth will also do.)
water		
handkerchief	3	Turn the woman's head to one side and place a cold, wet handkerchief on her forehead and cheeks. Keep the kerchief wet with cool water until the doctor arrives or until she regains consciousness, usually within a few minutes.
	4	If the woman regains consciousness before the doctor arrives, help her to sit up and give her sips of cold water. Explain that everything is fine and under control.
	5	Offer a shoulder for the woman to rest her head on until the doctor arrives.

GETTING YOUR FOOT IN THE BEDROOM DOOR

To get into bed with the woman of his dreams, a man has to know how to wait for the right moment. I've seen a number of guys try to get their foot in the bedroom door too early only to end up with broken toes.

You will need	**H O W T O**
date	**1** Asking a woman out on a date is a cinch compared to getting her under the covers. First you have to figure out a way to get inside her house. Suggest a nightcap after a night out, or mention that your malaria is flaring up again and ask for a glass of water.
charming anecdotes	
basic knowledge of women's clothing (specifically the bra)	
patience	**2** Once you're in, relax. Compliment her house and say how much you like her dog, even if the mongrel just peed on your foot, which may be a good excuse to take your shoes off anyway (one article of clothing down).
	3 Now's the time to start noting any subtle signs she might shoot your way. If she makes a drink for you but not one for herself and sits across the room with all the lights on and her arms crossed, you're probably off to a bad start. If she lights candles and sits beside you, hold on Nellie!
	4 Now is the time to stare deep into her eyes. Some men have been known to take a

continued on next page

continued

woman in one fell swoop with this brave tack. Others need to combine eye contact with the "lean-in". (This is when you pretend not to hear something she said and lean towards her saying, "I'm sorry. What did you say?")

5 So now you're kissing. That doesn't mean she wants to have sex with you, but a man can hope.

6 Let your hand wander to the buttons on her shirt and begin to unfasten them. She may at this point begin to unbutton your shirt. Let her.

7 To unclasp a bra with one hand, grab the strap on either side of the clasp between your thumb and index finger. While pinching the clasp rub your fingers in opposite directions from each other until the bra unhooks.

8 At this point your foot is in the proverbial bedroom door – you don't have to actually make it to the bedroom.

MEN
AT
WORK

Whether in the office, in the shop, or in the garden, one of the hallmarks of being a man is being able to do good work. That means he has to be able to accumulate the most expensive tools, cell phones, lap tops, and gadgets he can get his hands on. They make things so much more fun. After all, good work is not only work. It involves some play. You just have to know when to separate the two.

MOBILE PHONE ETIQUETTE

How many times have you wanted to clobber the idiot on his mobile in a restaurant or who is dumb enough to try and get on a busy motorway with one hand on the wheel and one on his phone? It's not just infuriating, it's plain rude. If you have a mobile phone, don't be one of these people.

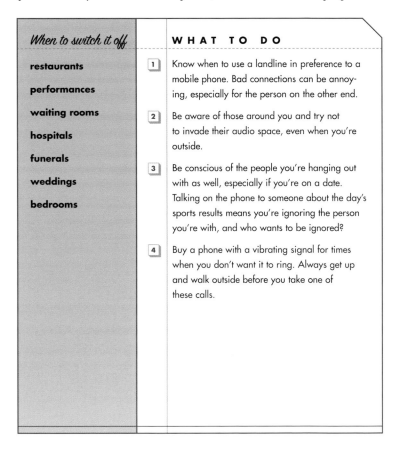

When to switch it off

restaurants

performances

waiting rooms

hospitals

funerals

weddings

bedrooms

WHAT TO DO

1. Know when to use a landline in preference to a mobile phone. Bad connections can be annoying, especially for the person on the other end.

2. Be aware of those around you and try not to invade their audio space, even when you're outside.

3. Be conscious of the people you're hanging out with as well, especially if you're on a date. Talking on the phone to someone about the day's sports results means you're ignoring the person you're with, and who wants to be ignored?

4. Buy a phone with a vibrating signal for times when you don't want it to ring. Always get up and walk outside before you take one of these calls.

EMAIL ETIQUETTE

Writing and receiving an email is very different from talking on the phone, but it's not quite like writing or receiving a letter either.

BUSINESS EMAILS

When a man goes to work, he should go to work. While you're in the office (or in the cubicle) forget all that instant messaging mumbo jumbo. And whatever you do don't email friends photos of barely clad women or the latest round of crude jokes. They could end up in your boss's in-box.

WHAT TO DO

✓ An email you send to co-workers or clients should be concise and to the point, but not so short that it comes across as rude.

✓ Skip abbreviations like plz and thnx and, unless you know someone pretty well, forget the little faces you can make with a colon, a dash and a parenthesis. :-)

✓ Also, avoid sending messages in all lower case letters. Doing that makes you look like you have no self-esteem (and girlfriends might think you're illiterate).

✓ Check spelling, grammar and punctuation carefully.

✓ Don't use your business account to send dirty jokes to your mates or sweet nothings to your honey. You don't know who is reading your mail.

DO'S AND DON'TS

✓ Do respond to emails, even if it's to say "I got it, thanks." Internet connections go down frequently and emails can get held up for hours. It's the cordial thing to do.

✗ Don't write in capitals. It is tantamount to shouting.

✗ Don't slag off your boss. That's just asking for trouble.

OFFICE ACCESSORIES

A desk with nothing on it means there's no work being done there, and that's not right. One thing a man should do if he's not working is at least give the impression that he's doing something. Too much stuff stacked up, however, and you'll start to look incapable.

WHAT TO HAVE

☑ Stress balls: Keep assorted shapes and sizes on and around your desk. If the boss objects, get the company logo inscribed on them.

☑ Remote-controlled car: This will boost morale (see Fig. A). One, called the Desk Rover, is a mini tank that can rumble over any stack of papers in your in-tray.

☑ Basketball waste bin: With one of these you can be like Mike Jordan when you throw stuff away (see Fig. B).

☑ Kinetic balls: Also known as Newton's Cradle, these are classic (see Fig. C). They are ball bearings suspended from a metal frame so that when you pull one back and let it go, the balls clickity-clack against each other forever.

☑ Stretch Armstrong: Make sure you get the original stretchy thing from the 1970s – with the cool hairdo.

☑ Sumo Wrestler Fan: The manliest desk toy around, this is perfect for those hot days when you're sweating over the paperwork.

Fig. A   *Fig. B*   *Fig. C*

READING MATTER

Reading is a great way to sharpen your intellect and bolster your libido. Friends will be impressed (and buy you cocktails) when they find you already have the latest guide to woodworking. And what woman can resist a man who knows his Heller from his Hemingway? It would take a lifetime to read all the fiction, biography and do-it-yourself you need, but a man's got to start somewhere. Here are a few essentials:

WHAT TO READ

- ✓ *The New Complete Do-It-Yourself Manual:* Reader's Digest.
- ✓ *Measure Twice, Cut Once: Lessons From a Master Carpenter* by Norm Abram.
- ✓ *How to Cook Meat* by Chris Schlesinger and John Willoughby.
- ✓ *Don Juan* by Lord Byron.
- ✓ *The Sun Also Rises* by Ernest Hemingway.
- ✓ *On the Road* by Jack Kerouac.
- ✓ *Moby Dick* by Herman Melville.
- ✓ *Ultimate Beer* by Michael Jackson.
- ✓ *Iron John: A Book About Men* by Robert Bly.
- ✓ *Waldon* by Henry David Thoreau.
- ✓ *The Worst-case Scenario Survival Handbook* by Joshua Piven and David Borgenicht.

LAPTOPS AND PALMTOPS

Owning a laptop can present a dilemma. It's one of the best toys a man can have but it does mean that, in theory, you can work anywhere you go. Same with a hand-held device. On the good side, though, with built-in calendars and relentless timekeeping ability, you should never miss an important date again.

LAPTOP

Buying a computer can be frustrating. Unless you buy the newest model with the latest processing chip you'll be out of date before the year's out. Then, once you spend the money updating you will have shelled out at least as much money as it would have cost you to buy the best one in the first place. So go ahead and get the latest and best right from the start.

WHAT TO DO

- ✓ Have an idea of what tasks you plan to do on the computer. If it's a glorified typewriter, then getting a load of graphics software bundled into the deal is a waste of time.

- ✓ Don't skimp on the size of the monitor. The bigger the better.

- ✓ Plan on buying a standard mouse to plug into the laptop because most of the built-in ones suck. The best are the mouse touch pads.

- ✓ How thin and heavy these babies are is a concern. If you buy into the lightest-is-best philosophy, what the hell: get the thinnest and lightest. If it's not that big a deal to you, losing an extra inch might not be worth the extra cost.

- ✓ Get a case along with an extra printer cable and an extra phone line that you can pack along with your laptop.

HAND-HELD DEVICES

If you keep missing important dates or can't keep up with your address book, a palmtop can help. These minicomputers are known variously as PDAs, palmtops or pocket PCs and have the ability to store thousands of addresses, log years' worth of dates, even play MP3 digital music files and video clips. Some come with a phone built in so you only have to keep up with one, instead of two, pocket-sized electronic toys.

WHAT TO DO

☑ The simplest and cheapest model will do, if all you want is to keep phone numbers and log important dates and to-do lists.

☑ Watching a video or listening to music is going to require up to 32 megabytes, and these also come with card slots to increase memory up to 64 megabytes.

☑ Pay attention to the battery life. Some may have to be charged more than others. Also, some will have removable batteries that you can replace once they wear out while others have built-in batteries that you're stuck with.

☑ Go for the black-and-white screen, unless you plan to watch videos on your palmtop. Then get glasses.

DO'S AND DON'TS

☑ Do keep owner's manuals handy for all your gadgets, and make a note of the tech support number.

☑ Do preventative maintenance by running regular disk scanning and disk defragmentation on your laptop.

☑ Don't be tempted to play with your palmtop in the bath (for obvious reasons).

☑ Do avoid spilling drinks, cigarette ash, food and other everyday detritus on any of your electronic toys.

SPORTS
AND
SPORTSMANSHIP

Those who think that playing or watching sports is a waste of time, and that the men who do the playing and the watching are a bunch of hard-headed jocks, have obviously never been on the winning side of a tough contest. Winning is not only about brute strength and unbound athleticism; it also takes brains, strategy, and smart decision-making.

HOW TO BE A GOOD SPORT WHEN PLAYING

Vince Lombardi, erstwhile coach of the Green Bay Packers American football squad, said that winning isn't everything; it's the only thing. But Lombardi, who was a gentleman and a scholar off the field as well as on (he taught high-school Latin, physics and chemistry before coaching), also realized the importance of sportsmanship. After all, victory is always sweeter if you practise hard, play by the rules and respect the competition.

WHAT TO DO

- ✓ Nobody likes to lose, but winning when you don't play by the rules is even worse. If you're playing an impromptu game on a playground make sure everybody knows what the rules are and stick by them.

- ✓ Also, anybody can win going up against a team of inexperienced 12-year-olds. Be sure to pick on somebody your own size.

- ✓ If somebody from the opposing team gets injured, don't stand there and celebrate. Lend a helping hand.

- ✓ When the opposing team or player makes a good play, let them know. This doesn't mean you need to be overjoyed. A simple "nice play" will do.

- ✓ Competition can really boost adrenaline and that can lead to angry confrontations. Try to keep your emotions in check. It's only a game.

- ✓ Finally, always congratulate the opposing team or player whether you win or lose.

HOW TO BE A GOOD SPORT WHEN WATCHING

Watching a big game on TV – like playing one – requires plenty of preparation. Before the opening whistle, beer must be stocked, food kept at hand, couch fluffed up and fresh batteries placed in the remote. The key is keeping interruptions to a minimum.

HOW TO

1. Before friends arrive, have crisps, pizza and other snacks out and ready to eat.

2. Consider filling a cooler with ice to keep beer cold and close by, instead of having to travel all the way to the fridge to get one.

3. Stake out your seat before everyone arrives and do not relinquish it. The spot should give you an unimpeded straight-on view of the action.

4. Keep hold of the remote. You'll want to be in control.

SPORTS FOR MEN...

When it comes to choosing a sport, ask yourself a few key questions. Are you a team player or do you relish the challenge of one-on-one? Do you like animals? And how good is your aim? Above all, make sure you opt for something that will make you stand out among your mates while impressing the ladies at the same time.

FOOTBALL: American, European, Australian Rules, Gaelic. They all take brute strength and tough heads.

RODEO: Cowboys who ride crazed bulls and wild horses have to be tough as nails to walk away from this sport.

RUGBY: If you can wear nothing but shorts and a shirt and throw your body into the path of an oncoming New Zealand full-back, you're either not very bright or you can take your licks with the best of them (which may mean you're not very bright.)

SKIING: Being able to fall down the side of a mountain gracefully takes a certain amount of skill.

SURFING: When man goes up against nature, it usually doesn't end prettily. Still, nothing beats the freedom you get from riding the big wave.

CABER TOSSING: This traditional Scottish game where large men in kilts try to see who can throw a telephone pole the furthest seems to be more about strength than strategy. It's good for those days when you don't want to put the thinking cap on too tight.

BULLFIGHTING: It takes some *cojones* to stand in front of an angry bull and thousands of onlookers with one of those silly hats on.

SHOT PUT: The only Olympic sport that allows men who weigh over 18 stone/100 kilos to wear a tight leotard in broad daylight.

...AND NOT

ICE SKATING: If you look like Fabio, it's a good fit. Otherwise, forget it.

GYMNASTICS: Although this sport takes lots of strength and balance, the bad news is that you have to wear those silly-looking tights to do it.

LAWN BOWLING: Is this really a sport?

BADMINTON: Great to keep the kids entertained, but there must be better ways to work up a sweat.

CROQUET: Not unless you happen to be drinking Slim's Gin and Ginger.

DIVING: Anything that forces you to point your toes is off the list.

TIDDLY WINKS: Two words that simply won't impress friends or dates.

POLO: It's not really a sport when you're just riding around on a horse, is it? Besides, how many men have a horse and a spare field they can use?

FITNESS

Inevitably you will want to get in shape for the summer months, and a man cannot get fit mowing the lawn alone (especially if he's opted for that mega mower). This means you are going to have to embark on some kind of aerobic exercise. This is not such a bad thing – unless you want it to be a bad thing – because the pain usually gets you motivated. A brisk walk for 30 or 45 minutes or a casual dip in the pool can burn as many calories as a two-mile jog. Plus, it's not nearly as hard on your knees.

AEROBIC ACTIVITY

This does great things for your body. It renews the blood and oxygen to your muscles and organs. It improves your physical stamina, lowers your blood pressure and helps put body fat to use. If you exercise regularly it will also help keep your spirits high while lowering your risk for depression, heart problems and cancer.

Walking, running, hiking, swimming, biking, rowing and even dancing are the tried and tested ways of getting a good aerobic workout. Health experts say that all of us should do one of these activities for 30 minutes each day, four days a week. The exercise can last the entire 30 minutes or it can be split up into two 15-minute sessions.

JOGGING: BEYOND THE BASICS

If you find that 30 minutes a day is too easy and you want to move on to a harder workout level, get yourself organized and plan out a weekly regime. But don't overdo it to begin with. You need to give your body enough time to rest and recharge between runs, or you may find yourself doing more harm than good. If in any doubt as to how much you can achieve, talk it through with your doctor first.

WHAT TO DO

1 Set a pace for yourself by slowly building up the distance you want to run. Go out for a brisk 45-minute walk, and start running when you feel like it.

2 Run for about 5 minutes and stop. If you run out of breath before then, slow down or stop altogether. There's no need to run too fast. When your five minutes are up, walk the rest of the way.

3 The next day, increase the time you run by 5 minutes. The day after that go 5 minutes more and so on, until you can run the entire 45 minutes without stopping.

4 If this is too strenuous for you, don't hesitate to change it. Some people stay at a 10-minute run for the first two weeks before increasing their pace. How far and how hard to run is always up to the individual.

5 When you get into a consistent rhythm, alternate days of hard workouts with easy ones.

6 Try to take a day or two off to rest your joints and feet. On those days, do another aerobic exercise, like swimming or bicycling, that is a little easier on your body but will keep you in sync with your regular aerobic workout.

7 Pay attention to what your body is telling you and adjust your workout accordingly. If you have consistent pain or soreness in a specific area of your body you may be setting yourself up for a serious injury. It's better to attend to those pains early on.

8 Time runs during the cooler periods of the day to give your body a better chance of cooling down.

9 Drink plenty of fluids before and after running.

10 Stretching before a run is essential to prevent strained muscles or other injuries.

11 Stretching after a run helps keep muscles from being sore later.

12 Don't overdo it.

GETTING THE PERFECT ABS

No question about it: men with perfect stomach muscles always get the best lifeguard jobs. Rare is the day at the beach when you see a water-rescue specialist with a spare-tyre gut. He wouldn't make it past the first wave.

HOW TO

1. If you're still eating a meatball sandwich with a side of Fettuccini Alfredo every night, no amount of stomach exercises will give you abs of steel. Getting a flat stomach is as much about eating right and having a good aerobic exercise routine as it is about doing sit-ups.

2. Once you get the diet and the aerobics under control, do a regular routine of abdominal crunches (a fancy way to do a sit-up) once every other day for six weeks.

3. Lie on your back on an exercise mat, bend your knees and put your hands behind your head.

4. Now lift your shoulders about 2in/5cm off the ground, exhaling as you lift up. Hold that position for a few seconds as you continue to breathe. Then let yourself back down to the mat. This is called a regular crunch.

5. For a full-body crunch, do the same as above except as you lift your shoulders, bring your knees in towards your chest.

6. Your daily workout should be 20 regular crunches and 20 full-body crunches.

THE RIGHT SHOE FOR THE RIGHT OCCASION

When it comes to buying trainers the more money you spend, the faster you can run and the higher you can jump. It's true. Just remember that you cannot afford to get caught playing basketball in a pair of jogging shoes. Only girls make this kind of mistake, and you will never live it down.

WHAT TO WEAR

- ☑ For jogging you'll need a lightweight shoe with lots of cushion and good heel support (see Fig. A). If you jog far – say 50 miles a week – the cushion will wear down fast and you may have to get a new pair of shoes every eight months or so.

- ☑ Hikers need good ankle support and a stiffer sole (see Fig. B). There should be plenty of room to wiggle your toes and the shoe should be big enough that you'll be comfortable wearing thick socks.

- ☑ Tennis players should have shoes that lend good support for side-to-side movement. If you're playing on a soft court – like grass or clay – choose a shoe with softer soles. Hard courts require a shoe with some traction.

- ☑ Basketball shoes should have thick, stiff soles and high top-ankle support (see Fig. C).

- ☑ For people who play more than one sport cross trainers are available. Most of these shoes provide lateral support as well as heel support and flexible soles for walking (see Fig. D).

Fig. A   *Fig. B*   *Fig. C*   *Fig. D*

A
MAN'S BEST
FRIEND

A man's gotta have friends. Who else is he going to show off his latest power tools to, or watch the Sunday football game with? Plus, a guy's buddies are the only people he can count on when times are bad. And if not? So what, get a dog. A canine comrade will always be there when you need him, even if you leave the poor beast out in the cold and rain for a night. Now that's friendship.

BOYS' DAY OUT

If you get tired of doing the same old things with your friends, and you can't find anything new to talk about, it may be worth a trip out to a local brewery. You'll be surprised to find that there is almost certainly one within driving distance of your home.

You will need	**H O W T O**
designated driver **some friends** **typed plan of action** **Rolling Stones'** ***Let It Bleed***	[1] When you plan out a day trip to your local brewery, make sure that they do in fact hold public tours of the premises and that beer-tasting is on the agenda. The last thing you want is for your mates to gang up on you in a Pavlovian frenzy. [2] Also, invest a little time and money in a few beer guides and familiarize yourself with brewing basics. Find out what ingredients go into beer and what the whole process involves. [3] When you're at the brewery sample each beer they offer. Most have beer tasters that give you about half a pint of each flavour. Also, listening to the history of the place will give you something to talk about the next time you're all together. [4] On the way home, listen to The Rolling Stones' *Let It Bleed* and rock out.

IRON-JOHN WEEKENDS

Sometimes it takes a weekend with your mates to really let a change of scenery sink in. Heading to the great outdoors is a good idea. There you'll find enough rugged adventure to keep everyone in his element.

Vacation ideas		HOW TO
white-water rafting and camping	1	No matter what outdoor adventure you choose, be sure to get in shape before you go. You don't want to a) get hurt and b) look like a wimp.
sea kayaking and camping	2	Get the right gear for the climate and terrain you'll be in and then get a couple of extras. There will be much comparison done and many judgements made on gear alone.
mountain biking		
mountain climbing		
canoeing and camping	3	Take a one-man tent so you don't have to share with anyone. After three days in the great outdoors even your best friend will start to smell bad.
overnight hiking		
sea fishing	4	On that note, cook beans or any other gaseous foods towards the end of the trip.
hunting	5	Stay up late around the campfire and tell stories.
road trip on motorcycles	6	Drink whisky, but only enough to warm your aching bones.

STAG PARTY DO'S...
...AND DON'TS

Ah, the stag party: an evening of ecstatic debauchery with the boys, justified no less, by long-standing tradition. Ever since the 6th century BC, when Spartan soldiers ate and drank to a comrade on the night before his wedding day, men have been blowing off steam before tying the knot.

These days stag parties have turned into much more than just dinner and drinks with the boys. Women – well dancers – are what usually come to mind when you mention a boys-only soiree for the groom-to-be. That and a lot of booze. But stag parties can be much more than an endless series of drunken lap dances. Some groups of guys organize two-day hunting, camping or white-water rafting trips. Others go gambling or hit the beach for the weekend. Remember: if you're the groom's best man, you're doing the organizing. Plus, you're in charge of making sure everyone has fun and doesn't get arrested during the party.

WHAT TO DO

☑ Plan the evening far in advance. First, make sure you know who the groom wants at the party and then make sure those people will be there.

☑ If you're going out to dinner, reserve a private room. A big group of guys in the main dining room of a fine restaurant will only be annoying for everyone else. Plus, it's a great place for a nice (or not so nice) lady to jump out of a giant cake and surprise the groom.

☑ Find a giant cake and a nice (or not so nice) lady to jump out of it.

☑ Collect everyone's money ahead of time and open tabs at the bars you go to.

☑ Tip your bartender well, and any other entertainers.

☑ Have fun.

WHAT NOT TO DO

☒ Don't have a stag party the night before the wedding. The groom will look and feel like a truck ran over him and wedding photos last a long time.

☒ Don't plan anything that is going to offend the bride. The groom will let you know if his fiancée is the type to laugh off a night with strippers or if that's something she doesn't like. This is definitely not the time for the groom to get into a situation that's going to compromise his relationship.

☒ If you're going to invite one person from the groom's office, you should invite everyone. But it's usually not a good idea to invite people he doesn't know that well, including people related to the bride. He wants to feel comfortable and probably won't be interested in small talk.

☒ Don't let everyone get too drunk too soon. Otherwise, neither the groom nor anyone else will remember what happened after 9 p.m., and that can lead to untold debauchery. The evening should be remembered until at least 10 p.m.

GETTING A DOG

Friends moving away? Can't keep a girlfriend? Going hunting? Get a dog. Canine companions will not only forever be at your side, but they won't care if you don't bring them flowers on their birthdays. They're also great outdoorsmen who will tramp through snow, icy water and rough terrain without thinking twice. Unfortunately, there are some dogs that don't even think once, and these fellas are as tough to handle as any bad tempered person. If you do get a dog, be sure to find one that will be an obedient companion as well as a good companion. And don't forget; taking a dog for a walk in the park is a pretty good way to meet like-minded ladies.

THE RIGHT DOG

COMPANIONSHIP: A dog that is the love of your life is a little sad. I mean, it's a dog. Then again, with a dog by your side you'll never be lonely, unloved or blown out. They're hairy and smelly but they're loyal to the end. Top breeders recommend: Labrador Retriever; Golden Retriever; Irish Wolfhound; Boxer; Doberman Pinscher.

SPORT: If you're into hunting, nothing beats going with a dog. They'll retrieve ducks in icy cold water. They'll show you where to shoot. Mostly, a good sporting dog is one that's been bred to follow a trail, hunt and retrieve with boundless energy. And for this reason they are not ideal for city living. Top breeders recommend: Pointer; German Shorthaired Pointer; Weimaraner; Coon Hound; Greyhound.

MUSCLE: Some dogs are pure brawn. They can be aggressive and hard to handle unless they're trained early and often. And then they can be sweet oversized puppies – at least to their owners. Intruders beware. Top breeders recommend: Rottweiler; Great Dane; Rhodesian Ridgeback; German Shepherd.

OBEDIENCE: There's a difference between a dog that's smart and one that's obedient. The Jack Russell Terrier for example is probably one of the smartest dogs out there, but is also one of the toughest to handle. It's almost as if naturally smart dogs can't be bothered by such sophomoric and tedious commands as "sir" and "stay". Dogs that are easy to train, on the other hand, learn how to be smart. Top breeders recommend: Field Spaniel; Australian Shepherd; Portuguese Water Dog; English Setter; Vizsla.

TEACHING AN OLD DOG NEW TRICKS

It is said that dogs obsess over their owners. They'll sit and wait for hours for you to come home. When you're home, they'll stand by your side and react to your every movement. Sounds cool, huh? It is, as long as you teach them that it's cool. Happy dogs are those that know what you want them to do. Unhappy dogs are those who are always being told no without being told why.

TEACHING A DOG TO SIT

Every dog should know how to sit. It's the first sign that you have a smart dog on your hands. Guests and dates will be duly impressed (and grateful that the beast didn't jump all over their expensive new clothes).

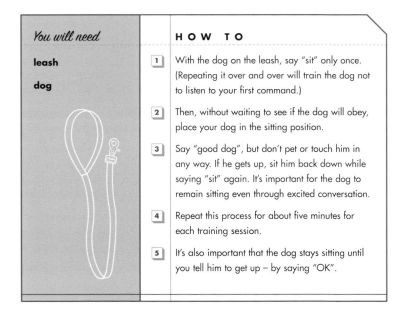

You will need	**HOW TO**
leash	1. With the dog on the leash, say "sit" only once. (Repeating it over and over will train the dog not to listen to your first command.)
dog	2. Then, without waiting to see if the dog will obey, place your dog in the sitting position.
	3. Say "good dog", but don't pet or touch him in any way. If he gets up, sit him back down while saying "sit" again. It's important for the dog to remain sitting even through excited conversation.
	4. Repeat this process for about five minutes for each training session.
	5. It's also important that the dog stays sitting until you tell him to get up – by saying "OK".

TEACHING A DOG TO FETCH

Most dogs will run and get something when you throw it. Most dogs will also never bring it back.

You will need		**HOW TO**
dog	1	Make sure the dog is on his leash and sitting.
dog's favourite toy	2	Throw his favourite toy a short distance away.
leash	3	Give the command "fetch" and let him run after the toy while still on his leash.
doggie treats	4	When he gets the toy in his mouth, lead him back to you and say "release". At the same time offer him a treat and tell him he's a good dog.
	5	Do not play tug of war with your dog and the toy. That will lead him to think you want to play that game. When given the choice of a treat or a toy, most dogs will drop the toy like a hot potato.
	6	Once your dog can fetch, replace the ball or stick with a rolled-up newspaper, saying "bring the newspaper" as you throw it.
	7	After two weeks of this, take him with you when you fetch the newspaper from the door mat in the morning. Ask him to bring the paper to you. When he does, take the newspaper from him and give him lots of praise and a treat.
	8	After about a week, you can ask him to bring the paper while you sit at the breakfast table.

HOW TO
BE A HERO

Every man wants to be a hero and, oddly enough, any man can. All you have to do is save someone from drowning, put out a fire, or scale a mountain. You know, simple stuff. And while these tasks may sound daunting, all it takes to do them is some preparation and common sense—two things that any man worth his salt is going to have plenty of.

BASIC FIRST AID

Being able to patch up a cut or treat a burn is simple and makes for good hero material. It's good to have a basic first-aid kit around in case of emergencies. Keep it in your car and pack another when you travel or go on camping trips.

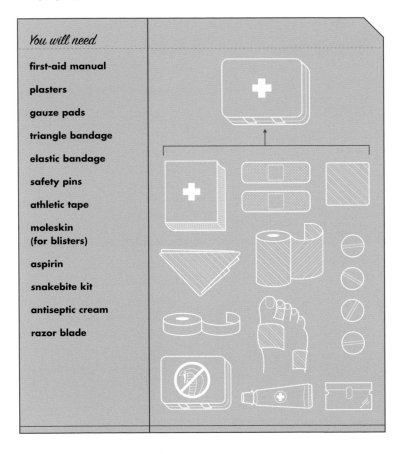

You will need

first-aid manual

plasters

gauze pads

triangle bandage

elastic bandage

safety pins

athletic tape

**moleskin
(for blisters)**

aspirin

snakebite kit

antiseptic cream

razor blade

BURNS

Cooking dinner for a pretty woman can make a man nervous, even if he's manning the barbecue. If you accidentally barbecue your hand instead of the T-bone steak, here's what to do.

HOW TO

1. Stick your hand in a bowl of cold water right away.
2. Hold it inside the bowl while the tap continues to circulate cold water around it.
3. Place a wet cloth on the burn until the pain goes away.
4. Use a dry gauze pad and athletic tape to protect the burn from scrapes and other things that might irritate it.

REMOVING A SPLINTER

Until your hands are callous from all the manly work you are doing around the house and garden, they will invite splinters, cactus spikes and thorns. Here's how to remove them.

HOW TO

1. Wash the area around the splinter with soap and water.
2. Sterilize tweezers by holding them over a flame and letting them cool down.
3. If the splinter is protruding above the surface of the skin, use the tweezers to grab it close to the skin and pull it straight out.
4. If the splinter is buried in the skin, use a sterilized needle to loosen the skin before using the tweezers.
5. Wash again with soap and water.

CUTS AND GRAZES

If a cut or scratch turns red and painful with some swelling and a collection of pus, then you've waited too long to care for it. Avoid infections by treating cuts and scratches right away.

HOW TO

1. If a cut is bleeding, place a gauze pad over the wound and apply direct pressure with your hand, or fingers, until it stops.

2. Then, wash the cut thoroughly (yes it's going to hurt) with soap and warm water. Make sure you get any dirt out of the wound.

3. Cover with a plaster.

4. If the cut is deep, get to a doctor as soon as possible.

BEE STINGS

If you spend a lot of time in the garden or if you have little boys who like to explore behind bushes and in trees, there will be bees. And where there are bees there are bee stings.

HOW TO

1. A bee will leave his stinger behind which, if not removed, will continue to release poison into the bloodstream. Remove the stinger right away by scraping it out with a fingernail or with the blade of a pocketknife. Do not remove a stinger with tweezers as this will squeeze it, releasing more poison.

2. Wash the area with soap and water.

3. To relieve the pain, apply a bicarbonate of soda/water mixture to the sting.

SNAKEBITES

If you know you're heading into snake country, it's always good to bring along a snakebite kit so that you can use the suction extractor that comes inside of it. Do not cut open the wound with a knife like in all those Westerns. You'll just have a snakebite and a knife cut to deal with.

HOW TO

1. It's important to work quickly. If you have access to a car, get the person to a medical facility right away. It takes about two hours for snake venom to start bringing on symptoms and by that time a doctor could be applying an anti-venom medication to the wound.

2. If you can't get to a doctor, or the victim is a child, quickly loosen any restrictive clothing and wash the wound with warm soap and water.

3. Let the wound bleed for about 30 seconds to get some of the venom out.

4. Wrap bandages 4in/10cm above and below the bite to slow the venom. This is not a tourniquet and should not cut off the blood flow; you should be able to fit a finger under the bandage.

5. Place the suction extractor over the bite and draw out the venom until there is no more discharge from the bite. If one extractor won't fit over both fang marks, switch back and forth, sucking for two minutes at a time.

6. Dress the wound with a gauze pad and tape. Immobilize the bitten area and keep the wound below or level with the heart to reduce swelling.

7. Head to a medical facility right away.

THE HEIMLICH MANOEUVRE

If you just spent three hours roasting a nice fat chicken, the last thing you want is for one of your guests to start choking on it. Invented in 1974 by Dr Henry Heimlich, this surefire way to unblock a choking friend's airway is now a worldwide lifesaving standard. If somebody starts to choke, they will be unable to talk, but they will motion to their throat with both hands. Give them the Heimlich manoeuvre.

You will need	**HOW TO**
two free hands	**1** Stand behind your unlucky dinner guest and wrap your arms around his or her waist.
sense of urgency	**2** Make a fist and place the thumb side of your fist just below the ribcage on the choker's abdomen.
	3 Hold your fist with your other hand and make quick inward and upward thrusts into the abdomen. Take care not to squeeze the ribcage with your arms while you're doing this, but focus the thrust on your hands.
	4 This should expel the offending item from the victim's airway. If it doesn't, repeat the process until the person is breathing properly again.

SAVE YOURSELF

☑ If a chicken bone gets lodged in your own windpipe and there's no one around to give you the Heimlich, you're going to have to act calmly and quickly. You can follow the same procedure as above, or try leaning over the back of a chair or the edge of a table, thrusting your abdomen against it until you can breathe easier.

DO'S AND DON'TS

X Don't squeeze the ribcage during the manoeuvre, as this could break a rib.

X Don't slap the victim on the back.

HINT

✓ It is possible to use the Heimlich to revive a drowning person. Lay the victim on their back and turn their head to the side so any water can drain out. Put one hand on top of the other and place the heel of the bottom hand on the victim's abdomen just under the ribcage. Lock your elbows and make quick inward and upward thrusts into the victim's abdomen until all water has drained from the mouth. At that point, it the victim is still unconscious and is not breathing, perform CPR until medical help arrives.

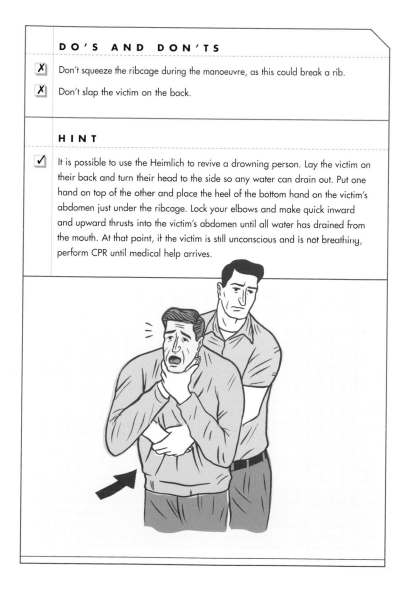

HOW TO RESCUE A DROWNING PERSON

Children who don't know how to swim fall into swimming pools. Rushing rivers can catch even the strongest swimmers off guard. Even your pet dog can get in over his head if he wants that stick badly enough. Once in the water, it can be a matter of minutes, even seconds before a victim starts to drown. Knowing how to save someone from drowning is essential if you spend any amount of time around water.

You will need		**WHAT TO DO**
length of rope	1	If the person is conscious and close enough to the shore or edge of the pool, lay on your stomach (to keep the victim from pulling you in) and reach out to them with anything they can grab onto.
towel		
long stick or boat oar	2	Talk to them and tell them in a loud, firm voice to grab onto the thing you're extending out to them. Once they grab it pull them to shore.
something that floats (Polystyrene cool box, spare tyre, pool float)	3	If they are further out, find something that floats to throw out to them. Life jackets, floats, cool boxes, the spare tyre in your car are all things that float and will work fine. If you have a rope handy, tie it to whatever you throw out so you can pull the victim back to shore.
boat	4	If they are too far out to reach with a stick or a float you can either get in a boat or, as a last resort, get in the water and swim out to them.
		continued on next page

continued

6. Be warned: people who are panicking and thrashing about in the water will grab whatever gets close to them, including your head.

7. If you do have to get into the water to save someone, swim up to them from behind while talking to them and trying to calm them down.

8. Grab the person's clothing or cup your hand under their chin and tow them to shore face up.

9. If they are out further still, get in a boat and make your way over to them. If you're in a small boat or canoe, don't let a panicked person grab on to the side. It will tip over. Also, don't try to pull a person into the boat with you. Instead have them hold on to the back of the boat and tow them to shore.

CARDIOPULMONARY RESUSCITATION (CPR)

There are many ways a person can stop breathing and his heart stop beating. Heart attack, near-drowning, choking, drug overdose and electric shock are just a few. When this happens you can keep a person alive with CPR long enough for professional help to arrive.

You will need	**HOW TO**
telephone	1. Call 999.
basic knowledge of CPR technique	2. With the victim lying on his or her back, tilt the head back, lift the chin and check for breathing by listening closely, while looking to see if the chest is rising and falling.
willingness to put your mouth on a stranger's mouth (possibly male)	3. Check to see that nothing, including the tongue, is blocking the victim's air passage, thus preventing them from breathing. If you see that they're choking on something, give them the Heimlich manoeuvre or clear the obstruction with your finger.
	4. If they're still not breathing, give mouth-to-mouth resuscitation. For this, the victim should be lying on his or her back, chin up.
	5. Place two fingers gently under the chin to keep the head back. Place your other hand on the victim's forehead, using the thumb and index finger to pinch the nose closed.

continued on next page

continued

6   Blow forcefully into the victim's mouth, making sure to cover the mouth with your lips so that no air escapes. You will be able to see the chest rise when you blow and fall when you stop. Repeat.

7   If the person is able to breathe on their own, stop. If not, check for a pulse by placing two fingers on the neck just to the left or right of, and slightly up from, the Adam's apple. If there is a pulse, continue mouth-to-mouth until the victim can breathe or until help arrives.

8   If there is no pulse, put the heel of one hand at the centre of the victim's chest, just on top of the breastbone. Put your other hand on top of it and interlace the fingers.

9   With your shoulders directly over your hands and your elbows straight, push down firmly on the chest by about 2in/5cm. Wait half a second and release. Repeat this 15 times.

10   After 15 pumps, give two more breaths. Continue 15 pumps and two breaths until help arrives.

D O ' S   A N D   D O N ' T S

X   Do not give CPR to someone who doesn't need it. You could seriously injure them even more than they already are.

✓   Do check frequently to make sure they're breathing on their own. If they are, you can stop CPR.

HOW TO STOP A FIGHT

Men are often called upon to do the jobs nobody else wants to do. They can be dirty, thankless and, at times, painful. Stopping a fight is one of those jobs. And yet, think of the dental bills and facial reconstruction costs you can defer by stepping between two flailing lunatics. Whether the fighters realize it or not as they're trying to rip each other's head off, you're saving them money and much more pain. So even though you may take a wild punch to the side of the face, you can feel good knowing your efforts helped in some small way.

You will need	WHAT TO DO
loud voice **bucket of ice-cold water** **two free hands**	**1** Before attempting to get stuck in yourself, try to separate the men by distracting them in some way. Things that have worked in the past are calling out their names (if you happen to know them) and throwing a bucket of ice-cold water over them. **2** If these fail, you'll have to grab the aggressor from behind and pull him away from the action.

DO'S AND DON'TS

✗ Don't jump into the middle of the fight, unless you are prepared to receive a few hard thumps for your interest in this scrum. Sure, you may get an elbow in the gut but this is part of a hero's pay for a job well done.

HOW TO PUT OUT A FIRE

Fires are bad news. They can destroy a man's hard-earned home improvements and they will wipe out his belongings. To squelch a blaze before it gets to that point, you have to deprive it of one of its three needed ingredients: air, fuel and heat.

You will need	**WHAT TO DO**
bucket	✓ If waste paper, carpet or wood is on fire, water will work fine.
water supply	✓ For electrical and kitchen-fat fires, use a blanket or sand to smother the flames.
blanket	
sand	✓ Fire extinguishers are rated by size and type of fire they can put out: Class A fires are those involving wood, paper, cloth, etc.; Class B fires are burning liquids, oils and greases; Class C fires are electrical fires; and Class D fires are those involving combustible metals.
fire extinguisher	
	✓ To use an extinguisher, point the nozzle towards the base of the flame and start spraying. Sweep the nozzle back and forth across the flame (always keeping it aimed at its base) until the fire is out.

HINTS AND TIPS

✓ Fire extinguishers have pressure gauges that need to be checked periodically to make sure they will retain enough pressure to push out the chemical fire deterrent they carry. After a fire extinguisher is used it loses all its pressure and needs to be replaced.

HOW TO CLIMB A MOUNTAIN

When Jacques Balmat and Michel-Gabriel Paccard reached the summit of Mont Blanc in the Swiss Alps, in 1786, with not much more gear than a homemade rope tied around their waists, the heroic sport of mountain climbing was born. And while they were clear about the route they took to get to the top, the two Frenchmen were a little bit more vague about what it took to get there. "It was a bitch", Balmat told his gastroenterologist some weeks after the ascent. He never elaborated.

Climbing mountains is difficult but not impossible work. Many peaks 14,000ft/4,000m and lower have well-worn hiking trails and can be accessed without any real technical skills. For higher peaks you will need a knowledge of rock- and snow-climbing and have a good understanding of cold-weather camping and survival skills. Also, mountaineering is not a go-it-alone sport. Take at least one partner if not a group. To get to the taller peaks you have to fill out lots of paperwork with the local parks department, including a detailed itinerary of your ascent.

You will need	HOW TO
medium- to heavy-weight hiking boots with ankle support **two sets of warm lightweight clothing** **four-season tent with guy ropes**	[1] Plan out your ascent and file it with the local mountain authorities. You should plan to stop 8,000 ft/ 2,500m above sea level for at least a full day to acclimatize to the thinner air and to avoid altitude sickness. Then plan to go 1,000–1,500ft/ 300–500m a day. Give yourself plenty of daylight time at the end of each day to set up camp for the night.
	continued on next page

continued

warm sleeping bag

camping stove

food that is high in carbohydrates

lots of water

outdoor survival kit

climbing rope

harness

crampons

ice axe

2. Start your hike slowly and go at your own pace. If fellow hikers pass you by, let them. This is not a race to the top. However, don't fall so far behind that you find yourself all alone. If you're hiking with a large group there should be a well-trained professional bringing up the rear anyway. He shouldn't leave you behind.

3. When you get above 8,000ft/2,500m it's even more important to go slowly in order to acclimatize to the high altitude. Hike no more than 1,500ft/500m each day, and drink plenty of water to offset altitude sickness.

4. Be mindful of avalanches and falling rocks. When crossing an avalanche field, walk quickly but not so quick that you'll lose your footing. Do not stop – even for a minute – in an area where there's been a recent avalanche.

5. When you stop for the night, pitch your tent. Then take off the sweaty clothes you hiked in and put on the second, drier (and warmer) set you have in your pack. Change back into the first set for the next day's trek.

DO'S AND DON'TS

X If you are having trouble breathing or sleeping at high altitudes or if you are light-headed, nauseous or vomiting you may have altitude sickness. Don't go any higher. In fact, it's a good idea to descend at least 1,000ft/300m and stay there to acclimatize for 24 hours.

MOUNTAIN RESCUE

A mountain rescue is not for the weak at heart. Nor is it for the wobbly kneed. Then again, neither is mountain climbing. To get someone off a cliff or down from the mountain after a bad fall, you'll need a sound knowledge of outdoor survival skills and first aid. Furthermore, it would not be a bad idea to have a sturdy grasp on how to use a climbing rope.

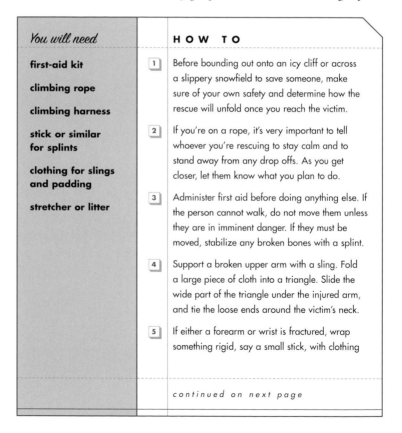

You will need

first-aid kit

climbing rope

climbing harness

stick or similar for splints

clothing for slings and padding

stretcher or litter

H O W   T O

1. Before bounding out onto an icy cliff or across a slippery snowfield to save someone, make sure of your own safety and determine how the rescue will unfold once you reach the victim.

2. If you're on a rope, it's very important to tell whoever you're rescuing to stay calm and to stand away from any drop offs. As you get closer, let them know what you plan to do.

3. Administer first aid before doing anything else. If the person cannot walk, do not move them unless they are in imminent danger. If they must be moved, stabilize any broken bones with a splint.

4. Support a broken upper arm with a sling. Fold a large piece of cloth into a triangle. Slide the wide part of the triangle under the injured arm, and tie the loose ends around the victim's neck.

5. If either a forearm or wrist is fractured, wrap something rigid, say a small stick, with clothing

continued on next page

continued

and tie it around the arm – either side of the injured area – with cloth strips. Then make a sling.

6   A splint for the lower leg can be made in the same way. Place a board or stick on either side of the leg – both extending from groin to heel. Pad the injury well and tie the boards in place at the groin, thigh, knee and ankle.

7   To transport a seriously injured person off a mountain, you will need a stretcher or litter along with several more ropes. Always move slowly and take the safest and easiest route down, not necessarily the quickest.

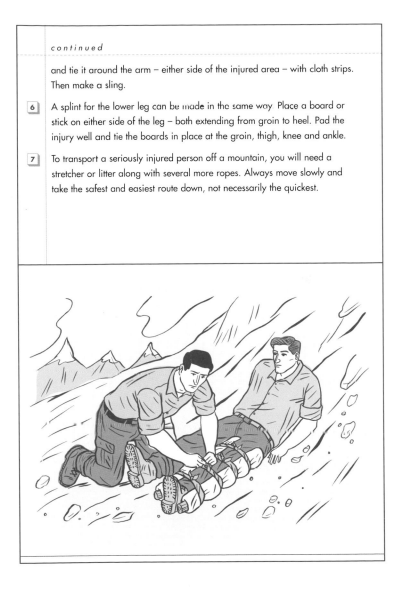

INDEX